OpenLinux:
An Introduction

Caldera Press
366 Cambridge Avenue
Palo Alto, CA 94306
U.S.A.

Copyrights

Trademarks

Contents

CHAPTER 3   *Installing OpenLinux* *25*

CHAPTER 6   *Working With Internet and Intranet Services.* *147*

APPENDIX A   *Hardware Parameters.* *161*

APPENDIX G *Configuring the X Window System 179*

APPENDIX H *Software Packages Index. 189*

APPENDIX I *Printing Usage HOWTO. 219*

Introduction

Welcome to the Caldera OpenLinux™ operating system, a complete
operating environment for your computer. *OpenLinux: An Introduction*
will help you install the CD-ROM of OpenLinux Lite included in the
back of this book, and then help you become familiar with Linux technology and the powerful features that OpenLinux products provide.

This book will also give you some information about installing and
running applications on your OpenLinux system.

About This Guide

This book is only a small part of the documentation that is available for
OpenLinux products. Thousands of pages of additional documentation
are available online after you install the CDROM in the back of this
book. After you install OpenLinux Lite, you can double-click the
Caldera Info icon on the Desktop to see a list of available
documentation. Links to many other resources are provided from this list
for those with Internet connectivity.

Some of the online manuals that are included with OpenLinux Lite are also sold separately as paper books. Check with your local computer book reseller or Caldera Press for availability.

This book is divided into several sections.

- Quick-Start Install

  Provides the most essential steps to installing the sample OpenLinux Lite system that is included on the CDROM in the back of this book. This Quick-Start chapter is intended for those with previous UNIX or Linux experience.

- What Is OpenLinux?

  Gives a description of the features and concepts that you'll want to know as you start to use OpenLinux.

- Installing OpenLinux

  Provides complete step-by-step instructions for installing the CDROM in the back of this book. When you finish the steps in this chapter, you will have a complete, working OpenLinux Lite system.

- Starting to Use OpenLinux

  Describes how to start using your new Caldera system, including starting the graphical system and some basic system administration tasks.

- Learning about the Desktop Interface

  Details how the Desktop interface operates, with examples of completing many common tasks using graphical dialogs.

Several appendices also provide more detailed technical information about the operating system.

The OpenLinux Product Line

The Caldera OpenLinux line includes several different operating system products, each with a different focus. OpenLinux is a technology core upon which Caldera's Linux Operating System products are built. The CDROM in the back of this book contains OpenLinux Lite. OpenLinux

Lite is a complete Linux-based operating system with the Linux kernel and all the standard UNIX utilities you will want to use to learn about UNIX and Linux, and create a working system. Many of these utilities are from the Free Software Foundation's Gnu project.

OpenLinux Lite includes a few commercial components like the Desktop interface and the CRiSP-LiTE graphical text editor. But these additional components are time-delayed. That is, after you have tried them out for a couple of months, they will no longer function. The complete OpenLinux operating system will continue to function, however.

Other OpenLinux products that you can upgrade to include features like the Netscape Navigator Gold browser with HTML editing, complete NetWare connectivity, personal-user office suite software, and the FastTrack Server from Netscape.

In this book, whenever we refer to OpenLinux, we are referring to the OpenLinux Lite CDROM in this book, unless we specifically explain a feature of another OpenLinux version. Still, many of the things you'll read here, especially about Linux itself, will also apply to all the other OpenLinux products. However, you should see the documentation for other Caldera products to compare actual features.

A Word About Copyrights

Caldera OpenLinux products are unusual among commercial software because they are a combination of software distributed under the Gnu General Public License (GPL), Berkeley license, other software that can be freely distributed (see the appendices for details); and copyrighted commercial components added by Caldera, Inc.

The software that is freely distributable includes the operating system kernel–Linux, and the utilities which accompany Linux, many of which are from the Free Software Foundation's Gnu Project. The source code for many of these components can be freely distributed, and is included on the OpenLinux Base CD-ROM. In accordance with the license terms, you can freely change and redistribute these programs. We recommend that you consult the license agreements beginning on page 233 to review which may apply to any code that you wish to redistribute; some freely available software packages cannot be redistributed without written permission from the copyright owner.

Caldera has included a Desktop interface, and other commercial software that runs with the Linux operating system. These commercial components cannot be freely distributed, but are licensed on a per-system basis from Caldera, Inc. when you buy this book. You must have a license for each computer that runs any of these commercial components.

Getting Help

In addition to the things you'll learn from reading this book, there are many sources of information about Linux and UNIX on the Internet (see "Where to Learn More" on page 22), Caldera provides several electronic resources to assist you with learning about and installing Caldera OpenLinux. Information that you can receive electronically includes:

- Technical support databases
- Updated hardware compatibility information
- Frequently Asked Questions lists (FAQs)
- Product feature summaries
- Pointers to newsgroups and Linux User Groups
- Updated or additional software components

Electronic Resources

The following email addresses will return an immediate automated response. The address *info@caldera.com* is also reviewed by Caldera staff, with personalized responses sent out as soon as possible (usually within 24 hours).

info@caldera.com. Use for general (non-technical) questions and comments on Caldera products. This address generates an auto-reply with information about how to contact Caldera and about Caldera products. Questions are answered by Caldera staff, usually within 24 hours.

faq@caldera.com. Auto-replies with a list of Frequently Asked Questions (and answers). Email sent to this address is not reviewed by Caldera staff.

majordomo@caldera.com. Auto-replies with information about email lists related to Caldera products, such as the *caldera-users* email list.

orders@caldera.com. Generates an auto-reply with information on ordering via fax, telephone, or email. Though not encouraged due to Internet security concerns, credit card orders can be sent to this address. A PGP key for order encryption is included with the auto-reply to this address. Credit card orders should include all card information (number, name on card, expiration); name, shipping address and phone number; and the product that you are ordering with the price you authorize for the credit card charge.

In addition to these email addresses, the following sources of information are recommended:

- World Wide Web

  Caldera's World Wide Web site, *http://www.caldera.com* can guide you through the many types of information mentioned in the previous section, as well as linking you to related Web sites and information sources. The Caldera Info icon on your Desktop includes a link to this Web site.

This Web site includes links to dozens of well-maintained Linux sites where you can get the latest information about Linux kernel development, device support, and user groups in your area.

- FTP

  Caldera's FTP site, *ftp.caldera.com*, includes all the online manuals, FAQ lists, release notes, updated programs, and known bugs list. In conjunction with the World Wide Web site, this is the best source of up-to-date information.

CHAPTER 1

Quick-Start Install

This chapter will get your new Caldera system up and running in about 30 minutes. To use the Quick-Start Install instructions, you should be familiar with common UNIX and Linux terms, and understand a little about computer hardware. If any of the concepts mentioned in this chapter or on-screen are unfamiliar to you, refer to the next chapter for more detailed descriptions.

You may need one or two blank, formatted, 3 1/2 inch diskettes to complete the installation. If you are installing across a network, you also should have your network and IP information before proceeding (IP addresses for node, gateway, and DNS server; hostname and domain name). The form on the next page provides a place where you can collect the information you need to complete the installation.

The Quick-Start installation creates a completely new system. If you have an existing Caldera or other Linux system, refer to Chapter 3 for directions on installing the OpenLinux Lite CD-ROM from this book while preserving important data from your existing system.

Installation Worksheet

Collecting the following information now will allow you to proceed quickly through the installation process.

TABLE 1. Information to Collect for Your Installation

What you need to know	Example	Value for your system
CD-ROM Drive, make and model*	Sony, cdu31a	
CD-ROM IRQ and port	15, 340	
Ethernet Card, make and model*	3com, 5c309	
Mouse, manufacturer (and model)	Microsoft	
Mouse, port used (ps/2, or a serial port number)	ps/2 port	
Graphics card, manufacturer	Mattrox	
Graphics card, model or number	Millennium	
Graphics card, memory size in MB	2 MB	
Monitor, manufacturer and model *or*	NEC MultiSync C400	
Monitor, maximum scan rate	76 MHz	
Modem, manufacturer and model	Hayes	
Modem, serial port used	COM 2	
Hostname for your computer	brighton	
Domain name of your network	caldera.com	
IP address assigned to your computer	192.168.12.44	
Network address of your organization or LAN	192.168.12.0	
Netmask of your organization or LAN	255.255.255.0	
Broadcast address of your network	192.168.12.255	
Gateway or router address (if you have one)	192.168.12.254	

TABLE 1. Information to Collect for Your Installation

What you need to know	Example	Value for your system
DNS Name server address (if you have one)	192.168.12.1	
Additional addresses for gateways or name servers (if you have more than one of either)	[same style as above, but you may not have a second gateway]	

Items in the table above that are followed by an asterisk (*) should be detected automatically by the installation program, so no information must be provided by you. However, if automatic hardware detection does not succeed, you may need all of the information listed in the table. In addition, hard disk information may be required in rare cases, particularly with very large (over 1 GB) or older model hard disks.

Preparing Your Hard Disk

To use the Quick-Start install, you should have a hard disk partition of at least 250 MB free for a default installation, and a second partition of at least 16 MB free to use as swap space. If you do not have these partitions set up, you will have the option during the installation to use the Linux fdisk command to modify your hard disk partitions.

If you have a hard disk with another operating system on it, and you want to share that hard disk between OpenLinux and the other operating system, you must change the partitions. In most cases, this involves backing up your existing system, re-partitioning and formatting your hard disk using a tool from any operating system (such as the FDISK command in DOS), and then restoring the original operating system before installing OpenLinux.

If you are using DOS and MS Windows 3.1 or Windows95, however, you have another option. You can defragment (optimize) the files on your DOS partition, (use the DEFRAG command in DOS), then use a utility called FIPS to truncate your DOS partition without erasing the existing data on that partition. The FIPS utility is located on the CD-ROM in the \COL\TOOLS\FIPS15 directory. Backing up important data from your DOS or Windows system is still recommended before completing this procedure!

If you have not done so previously, use fdisk during the installation (as indicated below) to mark a partition for OpenLinux as Type 83, Linux; and a swap partition as Type 82, Linux Swap.

Completing the Installation

Follow the steps below to install the included OpenLinux Lite CD-ROM.

If you have a bootable CD-ROM drive:

1. **Insert the CD-ROM in the CD-ROM drive and turn on your computer.**

    Continue with step 3 below.

If you do not have a bootable CD-ROM drive or are installing across a network via NFS:

1. **Use the Linux dd command or the DOS RAWRITE command on a running system to create a boot floppy from the images on the CD-ROM.**

    a. Insert the CD-ROM and a blank 3 1/2 inch floppy diskette.

    The install disk image is located on the CD-ROM at \col\launch\floppy\install.img

    b. For DOS, use a command like this:

    E:\COL\LAUNCH\FLOPPY\RAWRITE3

    Enter the path to the floppy diskette and the install disk image name when prompted.

    c. For Linux, use a command like this:

    ```
    dd if=/mnt/cdrom/col/launch/floppy/Install.img of=/dev/fd0
    ```

Depending on your hardware, you may also need a Modules diskette. You can repeat this process with the Modules diskette image located in the same /col/launch/floppy directory on the CD-ROM.

You can also start the installation directly from a running DOS system without using a boot diskette. For directions on this process, see the readme file in the directory /col/launch/dos.

2. **Insert the Install diskette in the diskette drive and the CD-ROM in the CD-ROM drive and turn on your computer.**

If you are installing over an NFS-mounted network filesystem, the CD-ROM should be inserted in the CD-ROM drive of the NFS server, unless you have copied the needed portions of the CD-ROM onto the NFS server's hard disk. You will enter the NFS server's IP address and the directory to install from during the installation.

3. **When the boot: prompt appears, press <Enter> to continue.**

Messages from the Linux kernel tell you details about the hardware it detects.

If you realize during the installation that your hardware is not correctly recognized, restart the installation and enter boot parameters at this point. (Boot parameters are listed in the Appendix on page 161 or in the Installation On-line Help.)

4. **When prompted, press <Enter> again to continue.**

You can review the kernel messages by pressing <Left-Shift>+<PageUp> and <Left-Shift>+<PageDown> to be sure your hardware was detected properly.

5. **Answer the on-screen questions about your system.**

Use the Kernel Module Manager screens and Modules diskette that you made (if needed) to be certain that all your hardware is correctly recognized.

If you need to review messages from the Installation process, switch consoles by pressing <Left-Alt>+<F8>. Use <Left-Alt>+<F1> to switch back to the installation.

If you need to review other things, you can switch to a new console with <Left-Alt>+<F2> or <F3> and log in as help. Advanced users can also log in as root.

6. Choose the "Change Hard Disk Partition Table" option (if needed) to use fdisk to change partitions or mark partitions with the correct types for Linux and Linux Swap.

7. Choose the type of installation that best fits your needs.

Several options are provided, ranging from a minimal running system or minimal recommended graphical system, to a complete development system. You can also choose the specific software packages that you want to install. This is only recommended for those familiar with Linux or UNIX.

Installing the software packages will take from 15 to 40 minutes, depending on the installation option that you selected, and the speed of your hardware.

You can add or remove any software package with a single command after your installation is completed. A list of available packages is included in the Appendix on page 189 of this manual.

8. When the packages have been installed, follow the on-screen directions to provide additional configuration information.

9. Follow the instructions on-screen to configure and install the LILO boot manager.

10. The installation program will restart your newly-installed system without rebooting.

11. Log in as root.

12. Configure your X Window System by entering the XF86Setup command to create a valid configuration file for XFree86.

Complete instructions for configuring the X Window System are included in the Appendix beginning on page 179.

CHAPTER 2

What Is OpenLinux?

The Caldera OpenLinux™ operating system is a complete multi-user, multi-tasking operating system environment that allows users to easily interact with networked resources on local intranets or the worldwide Internet. OpenLinux allows an unrestricted number of users to browse and publish information on corporate LANs and worldwide networks.

This chapter describes some of the key features of OpenLinux in more detail, explains some computing concepts that may be helpful as you install and use it, and lists where you can obtain more information about Caldera products.

Key Features of OpenLinux

OpenLinux is a *distribution* of the Linux operating system. A Linux distribution is a complete Linux operating system, with its associated utilities. There are several different OpenLinux products, each of which build on OpenLinux as a foundation and add additional features and functionality to meet the needs of a certain group of users.

The CD-ROM included with this book is OpenLinux Lite. It contains a complete Linux operating system, but doesn't have the commercial components that are included in other OpenLinux products.

Many of the features of OpenLinux are features inherent in Linux; others are found only in Caldera's commercial OpenLinux products. Features of the OpenLinux distribution of Linux (and of the CD-ROM in this book) include:

- High-speed networking with TCP/IP, the Internet protocol.
- Support for a variety of other networking protocols, filesystems, and networked operating systems.
- Support for hundreds of hardware components, including CD-ROM, multimedia devices, laptop computers, high-speed networking cards, and high-performance video graphics cards.
- An easy-to-use installation program, with menu-based configuration tools that use the same familiar look-and-feel.
- A POSIX-based multi-user operating environment with complete Internet connectivity tools, traditional UNIX® development environments, and a high-speed, pre-emptive multi-tasking architecture that takes full advantage of 32-bit microprocessors. Caldera includes support for both ELF and a.out binary formats.
- An unrestricted number of user accounts on each Caldera operating system, for use on a single computer system.
- Complete Internet integration, including servers for DNS/NIS (name services), HTTP (Web), SMTP (email), FTP, SNMP (management), PPP/SLIP (dial-in), NNTP (Usenet News), and many others.
- A complete Web server, automatically installed and configured by default, with the ability to host multiple domain names ("virtual domains," used to support multiple departments or companies on a single computer).
- Access to all of your existing systems as a client: UNIX, Windows NT, Windows95, and Windows for Workgroups 3.11.
- Ability to remotely manage UNIX systems via remote login on networked or dial-in connections.

- Ability to remotely access network resources without requiring a separate machine as a dedicated gateway.
- Ability to run many DOS and SCO UNIX applications at the same time your computer acts as an Internet gateway for your organization.

Adding Commercial Features to OpenLinux

In addition to the features listed above, Caldera has added components that are not found in other Linux systems, but are part of various OpenLinux products. These value-added features can make OpenLinux a complete environment for authoring, publishing, and browsing information on corporate or worldwide networks. Although some of these features are not included with the CD-ROM in this book, they are listed here for your information:

- A sophisticated Desktop interface can be used to view and manage file systems, including drag-n-drop functionality between applications and file types, default or user-selected click and drag-n-drop options, and configuration of the Desktop environment via graphical dialogs. The Desktop includes color wheels, action-sound defaults, layouts, icons (with editing), graphical preference selection, and much more. A complete chapter describing the use of the Desktop begins on page 73.

  The Desktop interface is included with the OpenLinux Lite CD-ROM in this book. It is a time-limited version, however, and will stop working 30 days after you install the OpenLinux Lite CD-ROM. (The OpenLinux operating system will continue to work; only the Desktop interface is time-limited.)

- The powerful CRiSP-LiTE text editor is provided as a default editor on the Desktop. Whenever you open a text file, it is displayed in CRiSP-LiTE, providing an intuitive interface to edit the file.

  CRiSP-LiTE is included with the CD-ROM in this book. It is not a time-limited version.

- Netscape Navigator®, the industry-standard Internet and Web browser, is included with most OpenLinux products. Netscape is used not only for Internet browsing, but is integrated as the online help and documentation viewer.
- Metro-X from Metro Link Incorporated is a commercial X server, allowing easy configuration of your graphical interface on a variety of popular high-performance video cards. For additional support, the XFree86 X servers from the XFree86 Project, Inc. are included as well, and can be installed as needed.

  Only the XFree86 graphics system is included with the CD-ROM in this book.

Concepts To Understand

As a full-featured, multi-user, multi-tasking UNIX®-like operating system, OpenLinux may present some concepts that are unfamiliar to you. This section defines some basic terms that you will want to know as you install and use the operating system.

Virtual Memory

Computers nearly always have more hard disk storage than RAM storage. But RAM is where programs and data must be stored while you work on them. Virtual memory allows the programs to think that they have at their disposal much more RAM than your computer actually has. This is done by automatically saving data to the hard disk when computer memory is full, and then swapping that data back into computer memory when it is needed again by a user or application.

For example, suppose you have 5 applications running at the same time, but you only have 16 MB of memory. When you load a large data file into your spreadsheet, part of your word processor document might be saved to a special place on your hard disk. When you start working on the word processor document again, it is moved back from the hard disk to RAM without the word processor application doing anything.

OpenLinux uses virtual memory to efficiently run many applications at the same time, and operate on large data files without running out of memory. The area on the hard disk that the virtual memory feature uses is called the swap area. This is described further below.

As for actual system memory (RAM), OpenLinux™ will operate well in 8 MB of RAM if you use only text mode, even if you have many users or remote terminals. If you have 8 MB of RAM, you should specify a large swap partition (see page 13). If you will be using the graphical Desktop metaphor, or other applications under the X Window System, you should have 16 MB of RAM for best results.

Swap Space

OpenLinux uses a separate partition of your hard disk to store information that is being temporarily swapped from computer memory to hard disk by the virtual memory feature. This partition is called a Linux Swap Partition. The size and speed of the swap partition affects the performance of your system.

You determine the size of the Swap Partition when you create partitions during the installation process. The Swap Partition should be equal to or larger than the amount of RAM (memory) that your computer has, but at least 16 MB. For example, a common system might have 16 MB of RAM; the Swap Partition should be between 16 and 32 MB. If you have a system with a very large hard disk, or you run many applications at the same time, you could make the Swap Partition even larger.

Any space that you include in the Swap Partition is not available for regular file storage by any of the operating systems running on your computer.

Shared Hard Disks and Boot Managers

A single computer can be used for both OpenLinux and other operating systems. Most users who use this feature have either IBM OS/2, DOS, or some version of MS Windows on their computer with OpenLinux.

When you have more than one operating system on your computer, you choose which one to use when you turn on or reboot your computer. A brief prompt asks which of the available operating systems you wish to start. This process is managed by a program called a boot manager. Boot managers are stored in the Master Boot Record of your hard disk or floppy boot diskette, or on the boot record of a hard disk partition. When you answer the boot manager prompt, the boot manager transfers control to the selected operating system to continue booting.

The boot manager included with OpenLinux is called LILO: the *LInux LOader*. LILO is configured and installed as you complete the installation.

If you have more than one hard drive, you can easily dedicate one to your OpenLinux installation and a second to another operating system. You still use LILO or another boot manager to choose which operating system to boot.

While using OpenLinux, you can access data on other partitions of your hard disk (non-Linux partitions), as long as they are using a supported filesystem type. The supported filesystems include HPFS (for OS/2), FAT (for DOS/Windows 3.1), VFAT (for Windows95), and many UNIX filesystems. For example, if you have OpenLinux installed on the second partition of your hard disk, and Windows95 installed on the first partition, you can log in as root and use this command to mount the first partition:

```
mount -t vfat /dev/hda1 /mnt/win95
```

Now when you use the commands below, you are viewing the root directory of your Windows95 filesystem:

```
cd /mnt/win95

ls
```

You can view, copy and create files in the Windows95 filesystem, but you must follow the limitations of the other filesystem (in this case, only 8.3 filenames can be used).

Hardware Parameters

The Caldera Installation program should determine what hardware you have and allow the installation of OpenLinux to proceed without problems.

Occasionally, however, the Installation program needs a hint to correctly locate and use your hardware. If necessary, you provide this help by entering *hardware boot parameters* or *kernel module (insmod) parameters* during installation.

Each boot or insmod parameter indicates a type of hardware (or other option) and one or more values that identify that hardware or option so that it can be correctly used.

Boot parameters are entered at the boot manager prompt, before the operating system (or the installation) actually starts. For example, at the LILO boot manager prompt, you might normally enter linux (or press <Enter> if linux is the default).

```
LILO: install
```

If you determine during installation that boot parameters are needed, you might enter something like this instead:

```
LILO: install cdu31a=0x340,13 eth0=11,0x260
```

This example indicates the addressing information for a Sony CD-ROM drive and an ethernet card. The equal sign (=) separates the parameter from the values you provide. Commas separate values given to one parameter; spaces separate multiple boot parameters.

Any boot parameters that are needed for your system are entered during the installation process and stored in the LILO configuration file. You don't have to enter this information each time you start your system.

Kernel module parameters or insmod parameters are entered during installation when you use the Kernel Module Manager to load specific hardware support. These parameters are often similar to the boot parameters, but may be slightly different.

A complete list of boot parameters and insmod parameters is included in the Appendix beginning on page 161. If the Installation program is not correctly auto-detecting your hardware, consult this list. To use these parameters, you may need to know information such as the IRQ interrupt and memory address used by your hardware. Consult your hardware documentation or call your manufacturer.

Graphical Display Technology

The XFree86 programs included on the CD-ROM in this book support a wide variety of video cards and monitors (see the Appendix on page 179). The X Window System (*X*) is the underlying graphical system used by Linux and the Caldera Desktop interface. X allows you to take full advantage of the capabilities of your video hardware, and to distribute graphical applications across networks.

The program controlling the X interface (called an X server) can be configured as part of the installation process, or immediately after when you start to use your system. Some Caldera products use the Metro-X server from Metro Link Incorporated as the default X server; the CD-ROM in this book uses the X servers from the XFree86 Project, Inc.

As described in the Appendix, if you do need to make alterations to the default X configuration or use the XFree86 servers, you may need detailed information about your video hardware. This information can usually be found in your hardware documentation.

The X Window System provides powerful capabilities not found on any other graphical system. For example, any graphical application can be executed on one computer and displayed on a different computer. In addition, the configuration of X allows software to take full advantage of the features of your graphics hardware.

Networking

OpenLinux includes a wide range of networking features. Networking is usually installed and configured as you install OpenLinux. To complete the network configuration during installation, you need your network information, including your IP address and router, and the addresses of your name server and network. (See the form on page 2 or page 27.)

IP networking information is stored in several different directories and files. These files are set up during installation. If you wish to change these file, use the configuration tools provided unless you are very familiar with networking. You can view the man page for many of these files (for example, enter the command man hosts). But if you are not familiar with IP networking, we recommend that you take the opportunity during the Installation process to install and configure your IP networking.

Hostnames and Domain Names

In a large network, such as the Internet, computers are given names as well as numbers (see "IP Addresses" below). Different organizations or companies on the Internet are assigned names for their networks. These are called *domain names*. Examples include *caldera.com*, *ford.com* and *mit.edu*.

Within a domain (for an organization or company), a system administrator or user can choose a name for an individual computer. This is the computer's *hostname*. The full name to reach that computer is a combination of the hostname and the domain name where that host is located. For example, if a computer is named *frosty*, and is part of the network in a company with the domain name of *caldera.com*, then the fully-qualified domain name (FQDN) to reach that computer is *frosty.caldera.com*. You select the hostname for your computer in cooperation with your system administrator. The domain name must come from the system administrator, or you won't be able to access network resources.

On the network, the hostname and domain name are easy for people to read and remember, but for the computer systems, they are mapped to numbers based on the Internet Protocol (IP), as described below. A name server uses the Domain Name Service protocol (DNS) to map between IP address numbers and hostnames and domain names.

IP Addresses

Every computer on an IP-based network (including the Internet) is assigned an address that allows it to communicate with other computers. This address is written as a set of four numbers that uniquely identify a single location on the Internet, and allow information from other locations on the Internet to reach that computer. Here are several examples:

- 204.141.89.7
- 137.64.1.1
- 137.64.131.7

During the installation process, you will be asked for several IP addresses (see the form on page 27). Your system administrator or Internet Service Provider will have these addresses.

An IP address allows you to reach the Internet through your Internet gateway or Internet Service Provider. It also allows others on the Internet to reach you. In some circumstances, IP addresses are assigned dynamically and you do not see your address information. This is most common when using dial-up services with SLIP or PPP (see "Using SLIP and PPP" on page 20).

Blocks of IP addresses are assigned to organizations. Within these blocks, certain addresses are used for special things like gateways and name servers. Your system administrator will have an IP number for your computer, and will have also have the IP address of the computers on your network that are used as a gateway and a name server. These IP addresses are requested during installation.

Using OpenLinux Around the World

Caldera OpenLinux products are available with documentation and computer interfaces translated into several languages.

There are also several places where options allow you to effectively use OpenLinux in other languages. These options are described below.

At the beginning of the Installation, you select a language for the Installation. You also select a keyboard layout appropriate to your computer. The keyboard you select is used during the rest of the installation and when you start to use your system after installation. During the installation, you also choose a time zone.

The Root User

The *root* user is a special super-user account. As on other UNIX-like systems, the root user has access to all files and devices. This access is required to do many configuration tasks, but can be dangerous for day-to-day work because the root user can access (and change) anything on the system.

After completing the installation process, you can log in as root to complete system administration tasks. Do not log in as root for your day-to-day work.

If you log in as root and start the Desktop, a set of administrative tool icons appears on the Desktop. If you log in as your regular user account, you can also use administrative tools by changing to root access temporarily with the su command and entering the root password. Type exit to return to your normal user status.

Setting Up User Accounts

OpenLinux is a multi-user system. Whenever it is started, you must log in using a valid username and password. The root superuser and one other user account are created during installation; you must create other user accounts. This multi-user system allows many users to access the system at the same time. Even if you are the only person who will use the computer, you still use a user account for yourself that is separate from the root account.

You can add new users anytime using the configuration utilities described in Chapter 4.

Using SLIP and PPP

The Serial Line Internet Protocol (SLIP) and the Point to Point Protocol (PPP) are protocols that make your computer a full peer on a network via a serial connection, such as a modem operating over a voice telephone line.

Any computer that can use a modem can access a remote computer as a terminal, sending keystrokes and receiving characters to display. This does not make a machine a "peer" on a network, however, because all interaction takes place at the remote computer. This is known as *terminal emulation*.

By using SLIP or PPP, your computer is seen as a separate computer on the Internet or other network. Instead of all program execution taking place at the remote site that you are logged in to, your computer can execute programs that access the network directly. This means that multiple programs can be connected to the Internet, for example, and graphical Web browsers can be used on your computer over your modem connection.

PPP is generally preferred over SLIP because it is more robust and allows multiple protocols to be used (not just IP). We therefore discuss only the specifics of PPP here, though many of the same principles apply to a SLIP connection.

To connect to a remote network (including the Internet) using PPP, the site that you connect to (your ISP, for example) must allow you to connect using PPP. This connection is different than the specialized connection protocol used by companies like America Online or CompuServe.

Base includes all necessary software, both to connect to a remote computer using PPP or SLIP, and to allow other computers to connect to your Caldera system using PPP or SLIP.

The basic steps to establish a PPP connection are:

1. Install a modem and determine that you can access it via the serial port devices (for example, as /dev/cua0 or /dev/ttyS0).

2. Call a remote computer or service provider that allows PPP access.

3. Run the PPP script to initiate PPP communications with the remote computer.

4. Wait a moment for the remote computer to initialize the connection.

5. Begin using your Caldera system as if you were connected to the remote computer or network via a standard network connection (such as Ethernet). For example, start using the Netscape Navigator.

You Internet Service Provider can probably provide you with a sample script to connect to them using PPP. See the appendices for more information about PPP.

Your Caldera system can also be used as a terminal server, allowing other users to call in and connect to your computer via PPP.

Using OpenLinux on a Laptop

OpenLinux can easily be installed on many brands of laptop computers. PCMCIA hardware and some of the unusual video hardware included on laptops are detected as part of the standard installation process.

As a general rule, laptops are more difficult to install than desktop machines because of the unusual hardware they include. A smaller percentage of peripheral devices is supported on laptops, and some brands may not be supported at all. Nevertheless, many popular brands (such as IBM, Toshiba, Micron, and AST) run OpenLinux very well, including the complete graphical environment. If you have questions about your laptop, consult the information pages on Caldera's Web site.

Where to Learn More

There are many ways you can learn more about UNIX, Linux, and Caldera products. In the sections below, several sources of information are outlined.

UNIX/Linux Resources

A multitude of Internet resources exist to help you learn about Linux. As Linux is a complex topic, you should not expect to be able to troubleshoot all aspects of it until you have studied quite a bit. Frequently Asked Questions lists (FAQs), and the resources below can help you increase your understanding of Linux.

Other information sources include:

- The Linux Documentation Project (LDP). Part of this large collection of documents on Linux is provided on the Caldera CD-ROM. The full LDP is also available on the Caldera Web site at *http://www.caldera.com/LDP/* or from the Caldera Info icon on your Desktop.
- Several Linux newsgroups on the Internet, including comp.os.linux.setup, which discusses installation issues.
- Dozens of local Linux User Groups. A directory is available online; see the Caldera Web site at *http://www.caldera.com/tech-ref*
- The *Linux Journal* is a monthly magazine with a variety of technical articles and case studies, as well as a consultants' directory. Call (206) 782-7733 or email to *subs@ssc.com* for information.

Caldera Resources

In addition to resources about the Linux operating system and related technologies, you may have questions about the components that Caldera has added to OpenLinux, such as the Desktop.

Information that you can receive electronically includes:

- Technical support databases
- Updated hardware compatibility information
- Frequently Asked Questions lists (FAQs)
- Product feature summaries
- Pointers to newsgroups and Linux User Groups
- Updated or additional software components

Electronic Resources

Each of the following email addresses will return an immediate automated response. The address *info@caldera.com* is also reviewed by Caldera staff, with personalized responses sent out as soon as possible (usually within 24 hours).

info@caldera.com. Use for general (non-technical) questions and comments on Base and other Caldera products. This address generates an auto-reply with information about how to contact Caldera and about Caldera products. Questions are answered by Caldera staff, usually within 24 hours.

faq@caldera.com. Auto-replies with a list of Frequently Asked Questions (and answers). Email sent to this address is not reviewed by Caldera staff.

majordomo@caldera.com. Auto-replies with information about email lists related to Caldera products, such as the *caldera-users* email list.

orders@caldera.com. Generates an auto-reply with information on ordering via fax, telephone, or email. Though not encouraged due to Internet security concerns, credit card orders can be sent to this address. A PGP key for order encryption is included with the auto-reply to this address. Credit card orders should include all card information (number, name on card, expiration); name, shipping address and phone number; and the product that you are ordering with the price you authorize for the credit card charge.

In addition to these email addresses, the following sources of information are recommended:

- World Wide Web

  Caldera's World Wide Web site, *http://www.caldera.com* can guide you through the many types of information mentioned in the previous section, as well as linking you to related Web sites and information sources. The Caldera Info icon on your Desktop includes a link to this Web site.

- FTP

  Caldera's FTP site, *ftp.caldera.com*, includes all the online manuals, FAQ lists, release notes, updated programs, and known bugs list. In conjunction with our World Wide Web site, this is the best source of up-to-date information.

CHAPTER 3

Installing OpenLinux

The steps on the following pages will install the included OpenLinux™ Lite CD-ROM on your computer. Before installing, the requirements and needed information about your system are reviewed. The preparation of your computer hard disk partitions is then explained (you may want to review the previous chapter if you are unfamiliar with partitioning). Finally, we take you step-by-step through the installation. The installation should take about 45 minutes, depending on the speed of your hardware.

Before You Install OpenLinux

This Caldera OpenLinux Lite CD-ROM can be installed on a variety of computers, as outlined by the requirements below.

System Requirements

Your computer system must meet the following requirements in order to install OpenLinux.

- A 32-bit Intel-based personal computer.

  This includes the following processors or their equivalents or compatibles: 386, 386SX, 486SX, 486DX, Pentium.

  Other processors are not supported in this release.

- A 3 1/2 inch floppy diskette drive.

  The floppy diskette is required to boot the enclosed Caldera Install diskette and complete the installation, *unless* you have a bootable CD-ROM drive or start the installation from a running DOS system.

- At least 8 MB of RAM.

  To use the graphical components of the Caldera system, 16 MB are recommended.

- About 300 MB of hard disk space.

  This free space should be divided into two partitions: one for the operating system, and one for the Linux Swap partition. Partitioning and Swap space are described in the previous chapter on page 13.

  Although 300 MB is recommended for the installation, you can use less than this if you choose one of the Minimal install options, or substantially more than this as you install applications such as WordPerfect for OpenLinux (sold separately).

  You can easily share a single hard disk between multiple operating systems. This is detailed in the previous chapter on page 13. Instructions for partitioning your hard disk are presented in the next section on page 30.

- A supported mouse and video card.

  These are required to use the X Window System and graphical Desktop. See the Appendix on page 179.

Information About Your Hardware and Network

While much of your system hardware can be auto-detected during installation, you will still need to gather some information about your system and your network. The information listed in the following form is described in more detail in the paragraphs that follow the form.

TABLE 2. Information to Collect for Your Installation

What you need to know	Example	Value for your system
CD-ROM Drive, make and model*	Sony, cdu31a	
CD-ROM IRQ and port	15, 340	
Ethernet Card, make and model*	3com, 5c309	
Mouse, manufacturer (and model)	Microsoft	
Mouse, port used (ps/2, or a serial port number)	ps/2 port	
Graphics card, manufacturer	Mattrox	
Graphics card, model or number	Millennium	
Graphics card, memory size in MB	2 MB	
Monitor, manufacturer and model *or*	NEC MultiSync C400	
Monitor, maximum scan rate	76 MHz	
Modem, manufacturer and model	Hayes	
Modem, serial port used	COM 2	
Hostname for your computer	brighton	
Domain name of your network	caldera.com	
IP address assigned to your computer	192.168.12.44	
Network address of your organization or LAN	192.168.12.0	
Netmask of your organization or LAN	255.255.255.0	
Broadcast address of your network	192.168.12.255	
Gateway or router address (if you have one)	192.168.12.254	
DNS Name server address (if you have one)	192.168.12.1	
Additional addresses for gateways or name servers (if you have more than one of either)	[same style as above, but you may not have a second gateway]	

Items in the table above that are followed by an asterisk (*) should be detected automatically by the installation program, so no information must be provided by you. However, if automatic hardware detection does not succeed, you will need all of the information listed in the table. In addition, hard disk information may be required in rare cases, particularly with very large (over 1 GB) or older model hard disks.

Additional information about the items listed in the table above is provided in the text below:

- Your CD-ROM drive should be detected and configured automatically. If yours cannot be, you will need to know the drive maker and model, and perhaps some information about how the drive is being used (which ports and interrupts the drive is using, or what type of controller it uses).

  If you are installing over a network, CD-ROM drive information is not needed. Instead, you will need the IP address and directory path to mount for the installation. When you get this information from your network administrator, confirm that the directory has been exported via NFS, so that the Caldera Installation program can mount it.

- If you are installing your Caldera system on a network, your Ethernet card should be detected and configured automatically. If yours cannot be, however, you will need to know the maker and model of your card, and perhaps the interrupt and port the card uses.

  For all network installations, you will need a set of IP names and address numbers as listed in the table in order to configure networking. If you are using an NFS server for the installation source, similar information about the NFS server will also be required. Most of this information comes from your network administrator, though you normally choose a hostname yourself.

  NOTE

  If you are using Token Ring network cards, information and hardware drivers are available on the Caldera FTP site, *ftp.caldera.com*. If you have additional questions, please contact *info@caldera.com*.

- Your monitor should support the highest resolution that your graphics card is capable of. If you are not certain of this, refer to the documentation for your hardware.

Upgrading an Existing Linux System

Caldera OpenLinux is a complete operating environment. However, some users may already have a stable Linux system that they want to upgrade to OpenLinux without starting from scratch.

While Caldera components can be installed on top of existing Linux systems, Caldera doesn't provide any support for those systems, and the information on Caldera's Web pages may not be very useful, because it is aimed at actual OpenLinux systems; your combined system with part OpenLinux and parts of another Linux system may be hard to piece together because of all the differences between available Linux distributions and filesystem structures. These differences might cause conflicts with Caldera packages.

The procedure outlined here is not guaranteed to work on your system. Nevertheless, many users have had success installing Caldera OpenLinux components on other ELF-based Linux 2.x systems. The procedure below outlines how to do this.

Please remember that the Caldera commercial packages, including the Desktop interface and CRiSP-Lite are governed by the Caldera license agreement. *They are not freely distributable.*

1. Locate a copy of the **rpm** utility on the CD-ROM under /col/bin.

    This file contains the RedHat Package Manager utility, which is used to install, query, and uninstall all software packages from the Caldera CD-ROM.

2. **Install this utility on your Linux system.**

3. **Review the man page for the rpm utility by entering this command:**

```
man rpm
```

4. **Use the rpm command to install, verify, or un-install the packages located on the Caldera CD-ROM.**

    A sample command to install a package might look like this:

    ```
    rpm -i calderadoc-1.00-2.i386.rpm
    ```

    A complete list of available packages, with notations about which packages are Caldera-proprietary, is contained in the table beginning on page 190.

Preparing Your Hard Disk

Before you install OpenLinux, you must prepare the hard disk of your computer. This accomplishes two things:

- Many users wish to use two or more operating systems on a single computer, selecting one each time they start their computer. This is easy to do with OpenLinux, as long as your hard disk is partitioned so that multiple operating systems can co-exist.

  The easiest way to share a computer between two operating systems, however, is to purchase a second hard disk and use it for the Caldera system.

- The advanced multi-tasking provided by OpenLinux uses a feature called a Swap Partition. This is a separate area on your hard disk that is not used to store your data files. Instead, the operating system uses it as a virtual memory storage area (see "Virtual Memory" on page 12). You must set up a free area on your hard disk for this Swap Partition.

The sections below describe how to prepare the hard disk of your computer in three different situations:

- A new computer, or one that will be used only for OpenLinux.
- A computer with both OpenLinux and a DOS or Windows system.
- A computer with both OpenLinux and any other operating system.

Preparing an Un-Shared Hard Disk

If the hard disk on which you will install OpenLinux will not contain any other operating system, you should divide it into two partitions: one for the Linux filesystem, and one for the Swap Partition. You can complete this task during the installation using the Linux fdisk utility.

The steps to follow to use the Linux fdisk utility during the installation are provided below. You can proceed now to the Installation section; you will be directed to return here at the appropriate point.

Using the Linux fdisk Utility to Prepare Partitions

1. After your hardware is recognized, choose "Yes" to set up partitions on your hard disk.

2. Select the hard disk device to partition from the list shown.

   The fdisk utility starts and a list of commands is shown on-screen.

3. Use the **p** command to see a list of existing partitions.

4. If any old partitions remain, use the **d** command to delete them.

5. Use the **n** command to create a new partition for your swap area.

   This partition should be between 16 and 64 MB in size, and should be a primary partition. To specify a size, you can enter something like this:

   +32MB

6. Use the **t** command to mark the partition that you just created as Type 82, Linux Swap.

7. Use the **n** command again to create a main linux partition.

   You can use the remainder of your hard disk space for this partition. It should be a primary partition also.

8. Select the partition that you just created.

9. Use the **t** command to mark the partition as Type 83, Linux.

10. **Use the w command to write your changes to the partitions and exit the utility.**

If any problems occurred, use the **q** command to exit the utility without saving any of your changes. You can choose the same menu item and try again.

Preparing Shared Hard Disks for DOS or Windows

On DOS or Windows systems, you can share the hard disk with a Caldera system without re-installing DOS or Windows. *You should still back up important data before using this process, however.* If you prefer, you can also use the standard instructions for sharing a system, as shown in the section below, "Preparing Shared Hard Disks for Other Operating Systems" on page 34.

To prepare the hard disk of your DOS or Windows system, you will:

- Defragment your filesystem.

  This moves all the data on your DOS system to one area of your hard disk. (Data normally spreads all over the hard disk as you use your computer.)

  A DEFRAG.EXE or OPTIMIZE.EXE program is included as part of most versions of DOS or Windows. If you do not have a Defrag program, or something similar (such as utilities included with PC Tools or Norton Utilities), you cannot use this procedure.

- Shrink your filesystem partition with the FIPS utility.

  The FIPS utility cuts off part of the partition used by DOS or Windows so that you have "unallocated" free disk space. FIPS does this without damaging the existing data on the hard disk. You then use the free space created by FIPS to create a Linux partition and Swap partition.

  The FIPS program is included on the Caldera CD-ROM. *Always back up critical data before using the FIPS utility.*

- Create the Linux partitions using the fdisk utility during the Installation.

Complete the procedure below immediately. Then start the installation procedure in the next section. At the appropriate point, you will be directed to create Linux partitions from the free space created below by following the steps in the procedure "Using the Linux fdisk Utility to Prepare Partitions" on page 31.

Preparing Your DOS or Windows Hard Disk

1. **Boot your computer to DOS or Windows.**

2. **Run the Defrag utility.**

    On most DOS systems, the following command will start the Defrag utility.

    C:\> **C:\DOS\DEFRAG**

    Optimization is a standard option for any hard disk on a Windows 95 system.

3. **Use the Defrag utility to do a complete optimization of your hard disk.**

    The data on your hard disk is represented graphically by colored squares on your screen. When the optimization is completed (this may take several minutes), you should see all of the data bunched up at the top of the screen (representing the first part of your hard disk).

4. **Exit the Defrag utility.**

5. **Run the FIPS utility.**

    The FIPS utility is provided on the Caldera CD-ROM in the \COL\TOOLS\FIPS15 directory. The following command will start the utility.

    C:\> **D:\COL\TOOLS\FIPS15\FIPS.EXE**

6. **Carefully follow the on-screen instructions for the FIPS utility.**

    The default installation of the OpenLinux Lite CD-ROM requires at least 300 MB of free disk space including the Swap partition.

7. **Use FIPS to adjust the size of the DOS partition on your hard drive by using the arrow keys on your keyboard.**

8. Press Enter to set the size of the partitions.

9. Confirm the reduced size of the new DOS partition.

    FIPS writes the new partition information to your hard drive.

10. Start the Installation procedure in the next section.

    During the Installation, you will be directed to choose a root partition for your hard disk. At that point, return to the procedure "Using the Linux fdisk Utility to Prepare Partitions" on page 31 for directions on creating the Linux and Swap partitions and marking them for use.

Preparing Shared Hard Disks for Other Operating Systems

To have OpenLinux share a hard disk with another operating system, follow these steps.

1. Use utilities that run on your current operating system to back up your system.

2. Using the hard disk utility that came with your current operating system, re-create the partitions on your hard disk.

3. Create a separate partition of at least 260 MB to be used by Caldera as a root Linux filesystem for OpenLinux.

4. Create another separate partition of at least 16 MB to be used as a Swap partition.

5. Re-create a partition for your current operating system.

6. Save your partition changes and restart your system.

7. Re-Install your current operating system into the new, smaller partition that you created.

8. Begin the Caldera Installation procedure below.

You will need to mark the new partitions as a Linux partition and a Linux Swap partition during the installation. When you are instructed to select a root partition for the Linux filesystem, choose the "Change Hard

Disk Partition Table" option and follow the directions below to mark your partition types using the Linux fdisk command.

Changing Partition Types Using the Linux fdisk Utility

1. After your hardware is recognized, choose "Yes" to set up partitions on your hard disk.

2. Select the hard disk device to partition from the list shown.

   The fdisk utility starts and a list of commands is shown on-screen.

3. Use the **p** command to see a list of existing partitions.

   You should have partitions created for the Linux operating system and Linux Swap area. If not, see "Using the Linux fdisk Utility to Prepare Partitions" on page 31.

4. Use the **t** command to mark the smaller of the new partitions as Type 82, Linux Swap.

5. Use the **t** command to mark the Linux partition as Type 83, Linux.

6. Use the **w** command to write your changes to the partitions and exit the utility.

   If you had trouble, use the **q** command to exit the utility without saving any of your changes. You can choose the same menu item and try again.

Installing Caldera OpenLinux

If your hardware is not correctly recognized during this installation, refer to the section "Hardware Parameters" on page 15, and the Appendix beginning on page 161.

The OpenLinux Install diskette is regularly updated with new and improved configuration and hardware driver information. Images of the latest diskettes are provided on the Caldera FTP site.

Follow the steps below to install the OpenLinux Lite CD-ROM.

Start Installation and Recognize Your Hardware

If you have a bootable CD-ROM drive:

1. **Insert the CD-ROM in the CD-ROM drive and turn on your computer.**

   Continue with step 3 below.

If you do not have a bootable CD-ROM drive or are installing across a network via NFS:

1. **Use the Linux dd command or the DOS RAWRITE command on a running system to create a boot floppy from the images on the CD-ROM.**

   a. Start your computer using DOS or OpenLinux.

   b. Insert the CD-ROM and a blank 3 1/2 inch floppy diskette.

      The install disk image is located on the CD-ROM at
      \col\launch\floppy\install.img

   c. For DOS, use a command like this:

      E:\COL\LAUNCH\FLOPPY\RAWRITE3

      Enter the path to the floppy diskette and the install disk image name when prompted.

   d. For Linux, use a command like this:

      dd if=/mnt/cdrom/col/launch/floppy/Install.img of=/dev/fd0

   Depending on your hardware, you may also need a Modules diskette. You can repeat this process with the Modules.img diskette image located in the same /col/launch/floppy directory on the CD-ROM.

   You can also start the installation directly from a running DOS system without using a boot diskette. For directions on this process, see the readme file in the directory /col/launch/dos.

2. **Insert the Install diskette in the diskette drive and the CD-ROM in the CD-ROM drive.**

   If you are installing over an NFS-mounted network filesystem, the CD-ROM should be inserted in the CD-ROM drive of the NFS server, unless you have copied the needed portions of the CD-ROM onto the

NFS server's hard disk. To use the NFS server, the directory on the NFS server must be exported, with access granted to the machine on which you are installing OpenLinux.

You will enter the NFS server's IP address and the directory to install from during the installation.

3. **Turn on your computer**

After a moment, an initial Welcome message appears.

A version number for your installation diskette is also shown on this screen. If you should have difficulty recognizing new hardware, a newer installation image may be available on Caldera's FTP site.

4. **Press <Enter> to continue.**

If you discover later during the installation that your hardware was not recognized correctly, you may have to start the installation again and enter hardware information before pressing <Enter> here. This is described in the section "Hardware Parameters" on page 15.

After you press <Enter>, a series of messages scrolls down the screen. These describe how your system hardware is being auto-detected by the Installation program. At the end of this list of messages, the screen pauses.

To review the auto-detection messages, hold down the <Left-Shift> key and use the <PageUp> and <PageDown> keys before pressing <Enter>.

5. **Press <Enter> again to continue.**

If you have Plug'n Play cards in your system, you can type pnp before pressing <Enter> to disable sound and Ethernet cards that may cause conflicts with the Plug 'n Play probing. If you do not have Plug 'n Play cards, *do not* type pnp.

After a moment, a list of languages appears.

6. **Select the language to use for the Installation.**

All screen prompts and messages, plus all <F1> help messages will be displayed in the selected language.

7. **Choose your keyboard from the list and press <Enter>.**

```
┌─────────────── Keyboard Layout ───────────────┐
│                                                │
│  Choose the country-specific keyboard          │
│  layout.                                        │
│                                                │
│   ┌──────────────────────────────────────┐    │
│   │   German keyboard map                  │    │
│   │ ░ U.S. keyboard map                    │    │
│   │   French keyboard map                  │    │
│   │   U.K. keyboard map                    │    │
│   └──────────────────────────────────────┘    │
│                                                │
│                ┌──────────┐                    │
│                │ Continue │                    │
│                └──────────┘                    │
│                                                │
│ ─ <F1> Help ──────────────── <Esc> Cancel ─   │
└────────────────────────────────────────────────┘
```

8. **After a moment, a Hardware Recognized list appears.**

    This list only displays certain types of hardware: devices using the IDE or ATAPI interface. You should use Autoprobing or the Kernel Module Manager described below to recognize all hardware that is needed for installation. For example, the CD-ROM drive and the hard disk on which you want to install OpenLinux must be recognized.

    a. If all the hardware needed for installation is listed, choose Yes and skip to the section "Prepare A Source and Target for the Installation" on page 40.

    b. Otherwise, choose No.

    You can autoprobe for more hardware if you do not know what hardware is on your system. Autoprobing should find about 85% of hardware.

9. **Choose Yes to start Autoprobing.**

    If your system hangs during autoprobing, restart the installation and choose No at this point. The Kernel Module Manager appears, where you can specify other devices without autoprobing. See "Using the Kernel Module Manager" below.

10. **Read the warning message about Autoprobing and choose OK to continue.**

During the autoprobing, you can view the messages generated by the system. To view the messages, press Alt-F6 or Alt-F8. To return to the installation program, press Alt-F1.

11. **Review the list of recognized hardware again.**

   a. If all hardware needed for installation is recognized, choose Yes and continue at the section "Prepare A Source and Target for the Installation" below.

   b. If all hardware is not recognized, choose No, all hardware is not recognized.

   c. Choose No to the request to start Autoprobing. Then follow the Kernel Module Manager instructions below.

Using the Kernel Module Manager

The Kernel Module Manager allows you to specify drivers that support your hardware, and add module parameters if needed. You can use the Analyze menu option to review hardware information that has been autoprobed by the installation.

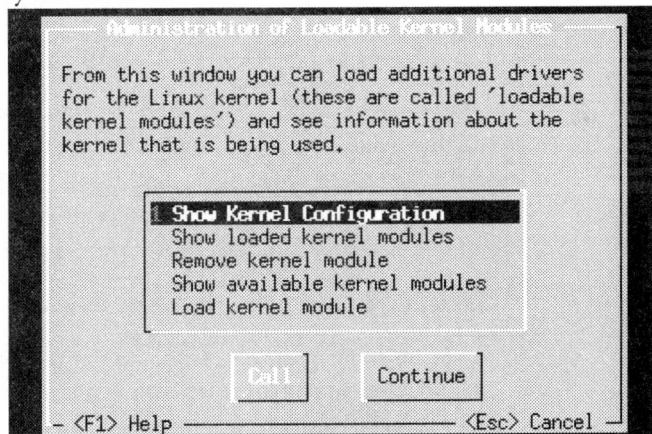

1. **Choose Load Modules.**

2. **Choose the type of hardware support that you want to load a driver for.**

   A list of modules appears.

3. If the module that you need is not listed, choose "Load More Drivers from Diskette."

4. Select the driver for the hardware that you want to load support for and press <Enter>.

5. If any parameters are needed to correctly recognize your hardware, enter them.

    The Appendix starting on page 161 contains a listing of insmod parameters that are used for kernel modules. They are also available in the online help by pressing <Alt-F2> and logging in as 'help.'

6. Select other hardware types or modules to complete loading for all modules needed to support your hardware.

7. When you have successfully loaded all needed modules, choose Finish from the main menu of the Kernel Module Manager.

    If you need to review the modules that you have loaded and how they are affecting your installation, choose the List of Analyze menu options in the Kernel Module Manager.

Prepare A Source and Target for the Installation

After you have correctly recognized the hardware on your system that is needed for installation, you must prepare and specify a place to install Caldera. The screen that appears after you complete the hardware recognition using the Kernel Module Manager or Autoprobing lets you use the Linux fdisk utility to prepare your hard disk for installation.

1. If you need to set up partitions on your hard disk, choose Yes.

2. Use the fdisk utility as described in the previous sections to repartition or set the partition types on your hard disk so that you can install Caldera.

    a. If you need to repartition your hard disk, refer to "Using the Linux fdisk Utility to Prepare Partitions" on page 31.

    b. If you need to change partition types, on your hard disk, refer to "Changing Partition Types Using the Linux fdisk Utility" on page 35.

When you change partition information using fdisk, you must reboot your system and proceed in the installation to the same point. This ensures that the hard disk information is correctly seen during the remainder of the installation.

3. **Select the correct partition to use as the Linux Swap partition.**

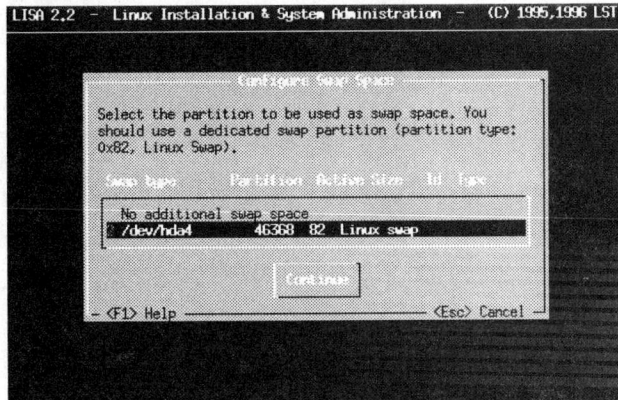

Swap partitions are described on page 13. Only partitions of the correct type (82) are listed to select from.

After you select the partition, an information screen tells you that the installation is preparing and activating the swap partition.

4. **Select the source to install from.**

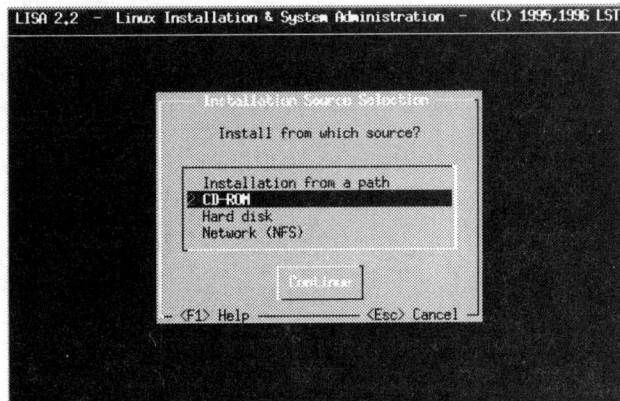

In most cases, the source will be the CD-ROM.

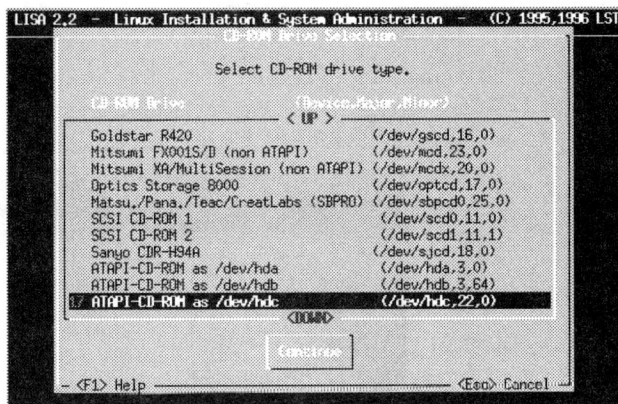

The CDROM drive detected on your system is the device selected in the list of CDROM devices. You should be able to simply press Enter at the screen above to continue the installation.

You can install from a hard disk if you have loaded the contents of the CD-ROM onto a hard disk on your system. You will specify a partition and root directory, which must correspond to the col directory on the CD-ROM. The bin, install, and data subdirectories from the CD-ROM must be included.

You can install via an NFS server where the CD-ROM or its contents are located. To use NFS, you must specify all the necessary networking information listed in the form on page 27, with information specific to the NFS server that you are using. The directory on the NFS server must also be exported, with access granted to the machine where you are installing OpenLinux.

5. **Select the partition on your hard disk where the Caldera system should be installed.**

The partition to install to must already exist and be marked with type 83. (The fdisk utility is used to complete these tasks.) Only partitions with type 83 or type DOS are shown.

6. **Answer Yes to the warning message about formatting the Linux partition.**

7.   Answer Yes if you want to check for defective sectors.

8.   **If you have additional Linux partitions that you want automatically mounted in your filesystem, answer Yes and specify them.**

In most cases, it is better to specify additional partitions after the installation is completed. Exceptions include when you want part of the initial system installed on a different partition, for example, the /usr directory could be stored on a different partition.

Select What to Install

After you select a source and target, you can specify exactly what you want to install. Several default selections are provided, or you can specify the exact software packages that you want. Each of the options is described below.

- Standard

  This is the default OpenLinux installation. It requires about 250 MB of disk space and includes the graphical Desktop, Internet servers, development tools, etc.

- Minimal (without X Window System)

  This is a minimal Linux system, with no graphical system. It requires about 35 MB.

- Minimal (with X Window System)

  This is a minimal Linux system, without development tools and many utilities, but including the graphical X Window System. It requires about 59 MB.

- Small standard

  This system includes commonly used utilities and the graphical X Window System and Desktop interface, but it does not include many development tools, additional utilities, or Internet services.

- All

  This option installs all the contents of the CD-ROM. It requires about 700 MB.

- Quick and Compact

This option allows you to specify groups of package that you want to install by the function of the packages. This is similar to selecting individual packages, but is faster because groups of related packages (such as games or text processing) can be selected together.

- Individual

  This option lets you select each package that you want to install. Packages are divided into groups like the Quick and Compact option, but you select each one that you want installed. When you use this option, packages marked with a '#' are required for an operational system. Packages marked with 'X' are pre-selected according to categories, but can be de-selected if you choose.

  This option is intended primarily for experienced Linux users. To use this option, carefully follow the instructions on the screen. You can even store your selections on a floppy diskette to use for installing multiple machines with a custom package selection. (You must have a Caldera license for each machine.)

1. **Select which installation option you want.**

    The default option is recommended for most users.

    If you select the Quick and Compact or Individual options, follow the instructions on screen to select the packages that you want to install.

2. **Press <Enter> to confirm the start of automatic package installation.**

    An information box appears showing you the progress of the installation as the packages that you selected are installed on the hard disk you selected.

During the installation, you can switch to a different screen by pressing <Alt>+<F2>, log in as 'help' and read documentation about the system or play a game of Tetris while the packages are being installed.

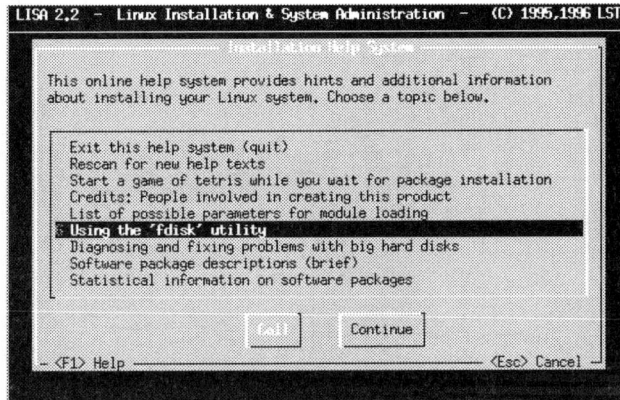

Final Configuration

After the packages that you selected are installed to your hard disk, you answer several more questions that you used to prepare configuration files for your system. These configuration options can be reviewed and changed later using the LISA utility.

1. **Answer each of the questions about the networking setup that you are using.**

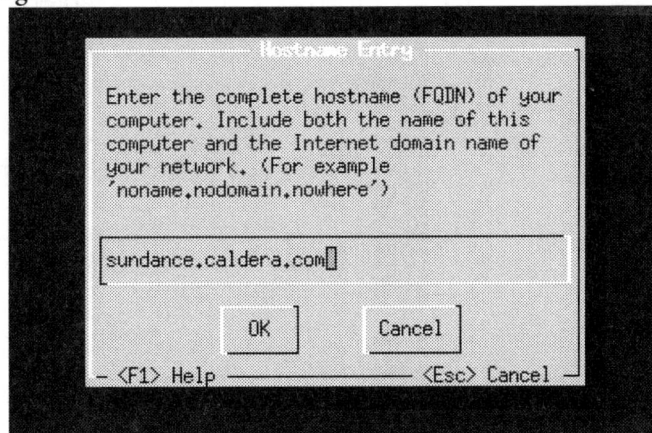

This includes providing the IP addresses and network domain and host-names that you collected using the form on page 27.

If you installed via NFS, you still must provide this information, because many people use a different set of network information for their NFS installation than for their day-to-day work.

2.   **Choose Local Time or GMT Time for your system clock.**

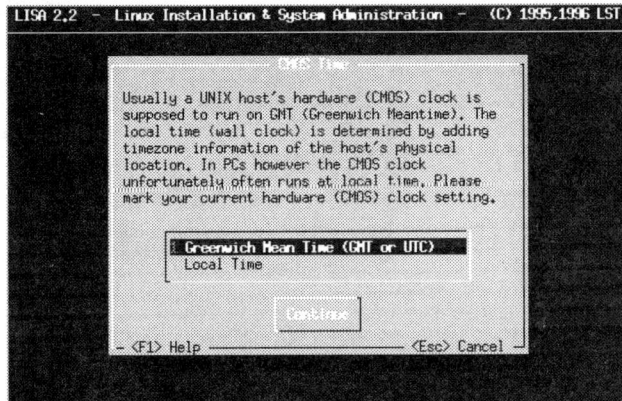

GMT (Universal Time) is preferred for UNIX/Linux systems, but if you have another operating system on your computer, GMT may cause problems. Use Local Time in this case.

3.   **Indicate your time zone.**

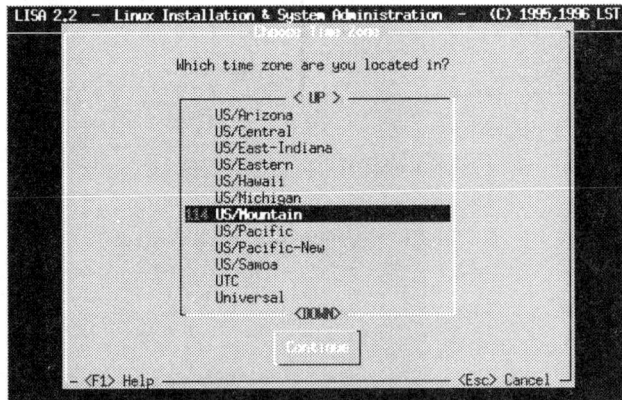

Time zones are arranged alphabetically. A GMT+ designation for the time zones is also included.

4. **Choose which brand of mouse you have.**

   This information is only used when running the DOS emulator in OpenLinux. You will specify and test your mouse settings again when you configure your graphical system (the X Window System).

5. **Choose which serial port your mouse is using.**

6. **Choose a printer driver for your system.**

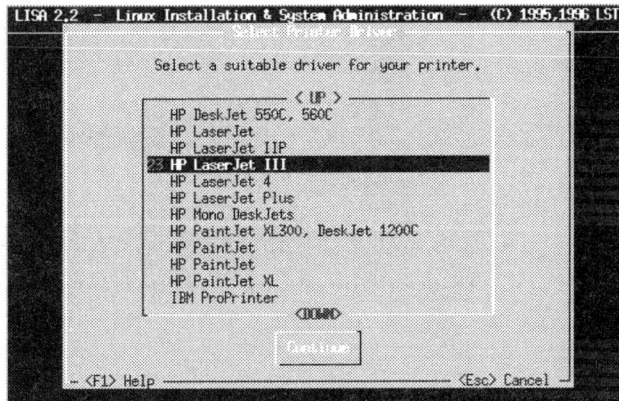

7. **Choose a printer port.**

   In most cases, this will be LPT1. Network printing is not configured at this point.

8. **Choose a default printer resolution.**

9. **Choose a default paper size.**

10. **Enter a password for root (the superuser).**

    You must enter the password twice to confirm that you typed it as you intended to.

    Do not forget this password!

11. **Enter a password for the new user account (username: col).**

You must enter the password twice to confirm that you typed it as you intended to. You should log in as user col when not completing system administration tasks. You can create other user accounts as needed with the adduser command.

12. **Select the CD-ROM type for your system.**

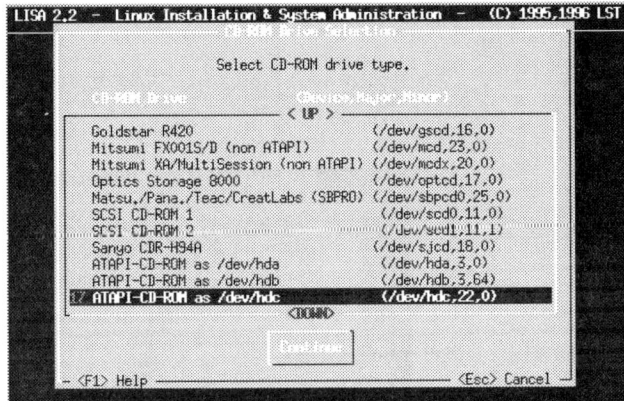

If you installed from a CD-ROM, this screen does not appear.

13. **Read the Boot Analysis information about your system.**

14. **Choose where to install the LILO boot manager.**

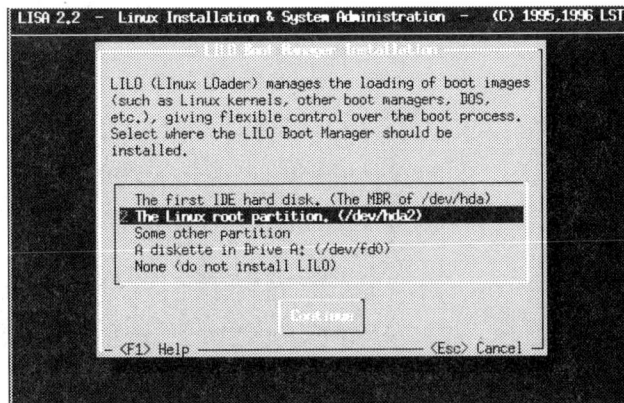

If you are uncertain where to install LILO, choose the default selected when the screen appears. It is chosen based upon the system analysis.

15. **Choose the image that you want to have booted.**

This is usually vmlinuz, a standard Linux kernel.

16. **Enter a label for the Caldera system you have installed.**

The common choice for this is linux.

17. **Confirm any boot parameters that you had entered earlier.**

These boot parameters are different than the insmod parameters entered in the Kernel Module Manager.

18. **If needed, add additional entries to LILO, such as a DOS partition.**

19. **Press <Enter> to confirm the installation of LILO.**

Several warnings may appear during the installation of LILO. In particular, if the hard disk you selected is not the first hard disk, you may see a warning message.

After LILO is installed, a message tells you of its completion.

20. **Press <Enter> to continue.**

21. **Select which X server to use.**

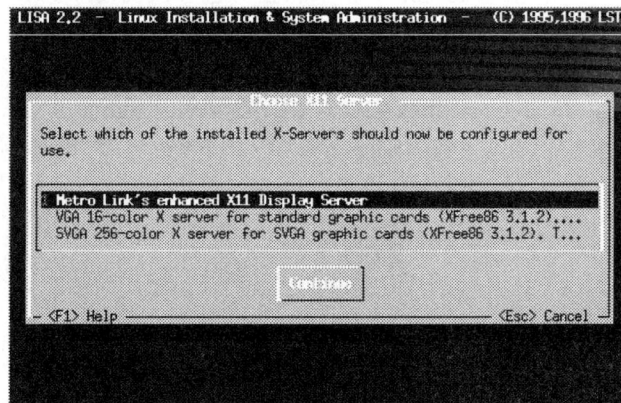

The standard VGA server for XFree86 is selected by default. It cannot be de-selected. You should also select other XFree86 servers, depending on what matches the video card in your computer. The SVGA server also supports many different video cards. You will use a graphical configuration tool to set up the X Window System after the installation is completed. Complete instructions for configuring X are included in the Appendix beginning on page 179.

22. **Press <Enter> to start your new Caldera OpenLinux system.**

    The installation is completed. Pressing <Enter> starts the new system without rebooting.

    The first time you start your system, several automatic processes begin indexing your system and updating new system files. Your hard disk will be quite active for the first hour or so of using your new Caldera system.

23. **Follow the instructions in the Appendix to configure the X Window System.**

24. **Turn to the next chapter to see how to start using your new Caldera OpenLinux system.**

Emergency Booting

After you have completed the installation, if you have trouble rebooting the system and getting back into Caldera, you can try the following:

1. **Restart your system with the Install floppy diskette that you made to start the installation the first time.**

2. **At the first prompt, instead of just pressing <Enter>, type the following, using the device name of your root partition (where you installed Caldera), in place of /dev/hda2:**

   ```
   boot root=/dev/hda2
   ```

CHAPTER 4

Starting and Using OpenLinux

This chapter describes some basic procedures related to starting and using your new operating environment. The procedures and concepts in this chapter include:

- Logging in and starting the graphical Desktop
- Shutting Down Your Computer
- Using the LISA utility for system administration
- Using basic UNIX command line tools
- Understanding the graphical environment
- Editing text files
- Adding and removing new software packages
- Working with users and groups
- Searching system help files
- Setting up initialization files

Logging In and Starting the Desktop

During the installation of OpenLinux, you entered a password for the root user and for a regular user called *col*. You should log in as user col or another regular user that you create if you are not completing system administration tasks.

To log in and start the Desktop, follow these steps:

1. **Turn on your computer.**

   A login prompt appears after the system boots.

2. **Type the username root and press <Enter>.**

   The administration tasks described in this section require that you log in as root. Normally, you should log is as your regular username.

   If you need to complete system administration tasks but have not logged in as root, you can change to the root user temporarily by entering the command su, and responding with the root password when prompted.

3. **Enter the password for the root user account.**

   For security reasons, the password does not appear on the screen as you type it in.

   A system prompt appears. This is called a shell or a character-mode terminal. From this prompt, you can enter any system commands, including the command to start the Desktop.

4. **Enter this command to start the X Window System and bring up the Desktop:**

   ```
   startx
   ```

   After a few moments, the Desktop appears. (If you did not choose an installation option that included the Desktop, a small toolbar appears instead.)

   Double-click on the README icon to review the latest-breaking news about this release of OpenLinux.

You can also double-click the Caldera Info icon to open the online help system. While using the Desktop, help is always available from the Help menu or by pressing the Help button in a dialog. (See the Release Notes for more information about using the Help system.)

5. **From the Desktop, choose Open Directory from the Windows menu.**

6. **Enter a directory name, then choose OK.**

   For this example, enter /etc as the directory name. As you use the Open Directory window, the Desktop will keep a list of directories that you have opened in the list below the entry field.

   When you choose OK, a Directory window opens. From windows like this one, you can view and manage your filesystem, and start programs. Information about using the Desktop to complete filesystem tasks is included in Chapter 5.

7. **From the Desktop, choose Terminal Emulator from the Run menu.**

   A text window opens on your Desktop. This is like the shell that you saw when you first logged in, but it can be resized, and you can have many of these windows open at once, running commands in all of them at the same time.

   If you have several Terminal Emulator windows open at once, your keystrokes appear in the active window. You select an active window by moving your mouse pointer onto that window's title bar and clicking the left mouse button.

8. **To close the Terminal Emulator window, enter the command exit.**

Using Several Character-Mode Virtual Terminals

While working in the Desktop, you may wish to perform some operations in a character-mode terminal like the one you saw when you first logged in. OpenLinux operates with six separate terminals that you can log in to and execute commands from.

Programs that you start in one terminal continue to execute when you switch to another terminal.

- Whenever you are in the graphical environment, you can switch to one of the character mode displays by pressing <Ctrl>+<Alt>+<F1> through <F6>.

- Whenever you are in a character-mode terminal (for example, after you first log in, before starting the Desktop), you can switch to one of the other terminals by pressing <Alt>+<F1> through <F6>.

- When you have started the graphical Desktop and switched to a character-mode terminal, you can switch back to the graphical display by pressing <Alt>+<F7>.

Shutting Down Your Computer

Because OpenLinux is a multi-tasking, multi-user operating system, you should never just turn the power switch off. You must tell OpenLinux that you are shutting down, so that anything that is still in process can be finished.

You can leave your computer on from day to day without concern. The screen goes blank if left unattended for a few minutes. You can turn your monitor off to save power.

When you do want to turn your computer off, follow this procedure.

Shutting Down OpenLinux

1. Exit the Desktop by choosing Exit Desktop from the File menu.

2. Exit the X Window System by holding down the left mouse button and selecting Exit Desktop | Quit Desktop.

    You return to the character-mode command line.

3. Start the shut down process by holding down the <Ctrl> and <Alt> keys together, and at the same time pressing the <Del> key:

```
<Ctrl>+<Alt>+<Del>
```

Messages begin to appear indicating that the system is shutting down.

4. **Wait for the screen to go blank, indicating that the computer is rebooting.**

5. **Turn off the power.**

If you do not use this procedure to shut down your computer, you risk losing data or damaging the configuration of OpenLinux. The next time you start your computer, it may take several minutes for the start-up process to automatically repair things that were left undone by suddenly turning the power off.

Using the LISA Utility for System Administration

Caldera OpenLinux includes a menu-oriented system administration utility that you can use to review or configure most aspects of your system. The utility is called LISA, for Linux Installation and System Administration. You should use LISA in most cases instead of directly editing system administration files.

You can start the LISA utility from a text mode or from a text window (terminal emulator) in graphical mode. You must be logged in as root to use LISA.

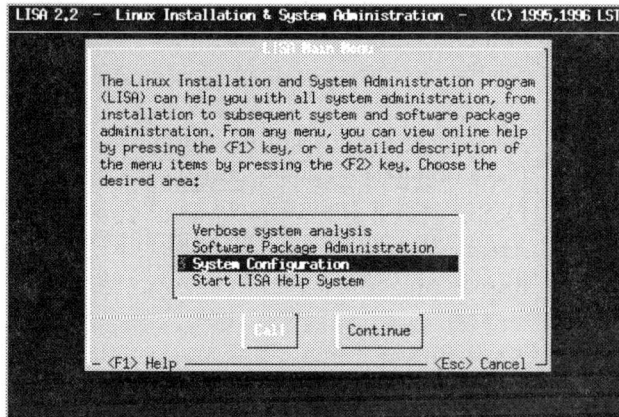

Once you have started LISA, use the arrow keys to select options, press <Enter> to choose the highlighted option, and <Esc> to back up to the previous menu. Use LISA for administering your hardware, network, or the software packaged that are installed on your system.

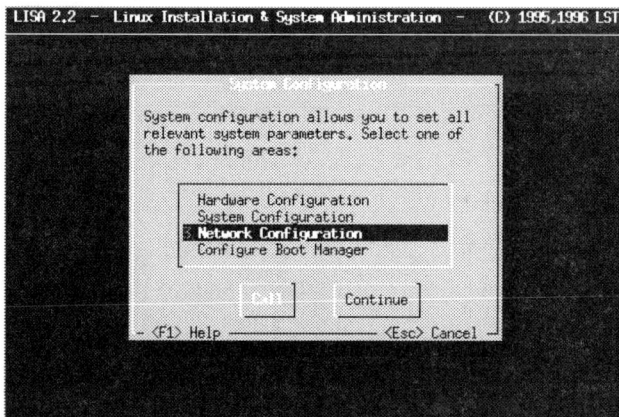

You can press <F1> at any time when using LISA to see a help screen for the current task.

Basic Command Line Utilities

Although the Desktop interface provides an ideal way to run programs, manage your filesystem, and browse network resources, you may still want to use the command line utilities to access parts of your system. Here we briefly describe several commands that are frequently used.

Many of the more advanced concepts and tasks relating to your filesystem and system administration are usually completed from the Desktop, and are discussed in Chapter 5. These include things such as setting file access permissions, creating symbolic links, and adjusting display preferences for the Desktop.

The commands below can be used from the character-mode command line, or from within a Terminal Emulator window on the Desktop. The commands are the same as those on nearly any other UNIX operating system, and are similar to many commands that you may be familiar with from DOS. Remember, however, that all commands are *case sensitive*.

TABLE 3. Basic Command Line Utilities

Command	Purpose
ls	List the contents of a directory (like the DOS command DIR)
cd	change to a new directory
pwd	Print the directory that you are in (called the Working Directory)
mkdir	Create a new directory
rmdir	Remove a directory
rm	Erase a file (like the DOS command DEL)
cp	Copy a file
more	Show the contents of a text file on the screen, pausing after each screenful until a key is pressed (like using TYPE *file* | MORE in DOS)
<Ctrl>+c	Stop whatever command is being used (Break)

To learn about a command, read the manual page or the help screen for that command by entering one of these commands.

```
man commandname

commandname --help
```

Here are some examples of the commands listed in the table above.

The command below lists all file in the current directory. The -l option shows additional information about each file, such as its size and owner.

```
ls -l
```

The command below prints the contents of the text file readme.txt to the screen, pausing after each screenful until a key is pressed. If the text file were long, you could cancel the command by pressing <Ctrl>+c at any time.

```
more readme.txt
```

To learn more about the commands available on your Caldera system and how to use them, consult the online *Linux Installation and Getting Started Guide.* You can access this document from the Caldera Info icon on your Desktop.

Understanding the Graphical Environment

OpenLinux uses the X Window System, often called "X," to provide a powerful, distributed graphical environment. Below are basic concepts to get you started using this graphical environment.

X and the Desktop

The X Window System is a graphical subsystem on which X applications run. The Desktop interface provided on your Caldera system is simply an application that uses the X Window System. As configured in OpenLinux, when you Exit the Desktop (by choosing Exit Desktop from the File menu), the X Window System remains open. From the blank X Window screen, you can see a menu of options by holding down the left mouse button.

The Desktop provides a convenient graphical method of interacting with, viewing, and configuring your filesystem and other computer resources.

Multiuser and Multitasking

The X Window System is a distributed, multiuser, multitasking graphical environment. It relies on the underlying Linux operating system for its functionality, but provides a graphical interface to use the capabilities of Linux.

As with Linux itself, you can have many applications running at the same time. They all continue operating simultaneously. If you have X terminals connected to the same network as the computer running OpenLinux, many users can each be using several graphical applications at the same time. The only limitations are how fast your machine is, and how much disk space, swap partition space, and memory you have.

Using Graphical Windows

When you have several graphical applications running on your Desktop, one application at a time has "focus." You can give focus to another window by placing the mouse pointer on that window's title bar and clicking the left mouse button. The Title bar and border of the application with focus changes color. Your keystrokes are sent to the application which has focus, even if a part of the window is covered.

- To bring an application window to the front, so that no other windows cover part of it, click the mouse pointer on the Title bar of the application that you want to use.

- You can resize a window by placing the mouse pointer in any corner of the window, or on the edge of the window. When the pointer changes to an arrow, you can click and drag the border of the window to resize it. Some windows do not allow resizing.

- To move a window to a new location on the screen, click on the title bar. Drag the window to a new location and release the mouse button.

- To close a window, you can double-click in the upper-left corner box, or click once in that box and choose Close.

Terminal Emulator Windows

While you are in X, you may need to enter commands to start applications or complete administration tasks. You can always open a Terminal Emulator Window, which is a command-line interface to the operating system. From this window, you can use command line utilities or start applications.

You can easily open a terminal emulator window at any time:

- Click the right mouse button on a blank area of the Desktop and select Terminal Emulator from the menu.
- Choose the Terminal Emulator icon on the icon bar.
- Choose Terminal Emulator from the Run menu of the Desktop.

The Window Manager

X uses a window manager to create and display the windows that you see on the screen. Many window managers are available for X. Windows appear slightly different under different window managers. The concepts below describe the fvwm window manager provided with OpenLinux.

Every window in X has some common functionality and controls that allow you to work with different applications in the same way. These parts of a window are:

- Title bar

  The frame outlining the window contains a title bar in its top border. The title bar indicates the application name and sometimes the document that is being used in that window.

- The Minimize and Maximize buttons

Located in the upper right corner of the window, the minimize button reduces the window to a small icon at the right edge of your screen (the icon may not appear immediately). The application running in that window continues to run, but the window is not visible. You can restore the window to its previous size by clicking on the icon for the window.

The maximize button causes the window to resize to fill your screen. Once the window has been maximized, choosing the maximize button again will restore the window to its previous size.

Right-clicking on the maximize button of a window that is not maximized expands the window vertically while keeping the same width.

- The Control Menu

   In the upper left corner of each window is a button which, when selected, displays a control menu for that window. The control menu allows you to resize the window, minimize it, maximize it, or close it.

The Desktop

The Desktop interface is an X application which is installed as part of the default system with OpenLinux. It can provide a full screen interface to your system and your other applications.

The Desktop area provides a space where you can place applications, commonly accessed files, or other utilities. Once these are on the Desktop, you can choose them at any time.

Online help for the Desktop interface is available by choosing an item from the Help menu or by choosing a Help button in a Desktop dialog. (See the Release Notes for more information about using the Help system.)

Directory Windows

From the Desktop, you can view and manage your file system by opening Directory Windows. Each Directory Window contains icons for directories and files. Icons are assigned based on the type of each directory and file.

Many Directory Windows can be opened at the same time, and you can intelligently drag and drop files and directories between Directory Windows, or to and from the Desktop.

Complete information about the Desktop is available online by choosing the information icons that are installed by default on the Desktop. The Desktop Help Screens contain information on using dialogs and menus. The Desktop User Guide contains more technical information on editing icons, assigning icons to files, layouts, and so forth.

Editing Text Files

Caldera OpenLinux includes a powerful text editor that you can use to work with all types of text files. The editor is CRiSP-LiTE, a pared-down version of the popular CRiSP editor from Vital Corp. This editor includes full keyboard and mouse control, drop-down menus, online help, and an icon bar of common functions, in addition to many more advanced features used by programmers.

CRiSP-LiTE is the default text editor for the Desktop. That means that whenever you see an icon for a text file on the Desktop or in a Directory

Window, you can double-click on that file to edit it. CRiSP-LiTE will open with that file, ready to edit

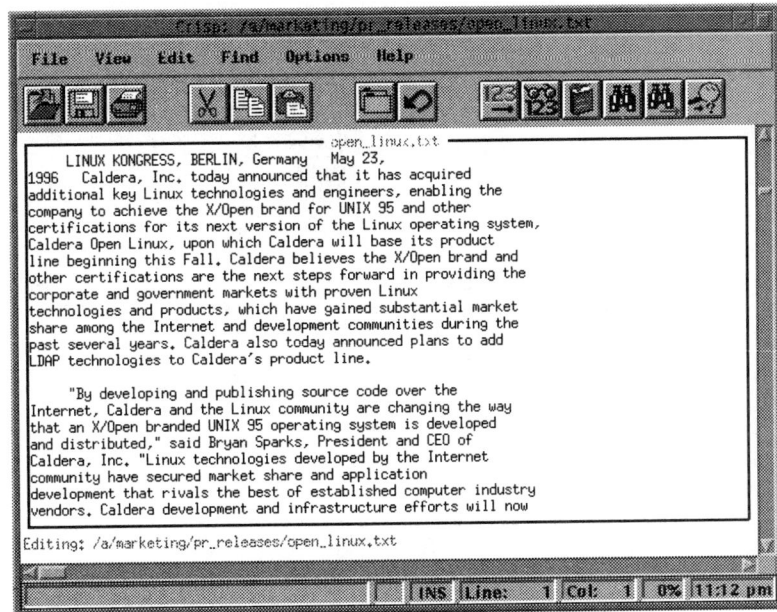

In addition, the icon for CRiSP-LiTE is on the Desktop by default. You can drag and drop any text file onto the CRiSP-LiTE icon to open CRiSP-LiTE with that file. If you double-click on the CRiSP-LiTE icon, the editor will open with no file.

NOTE

If you would like to change the default text editor to vi or emacs, see "Changing Execution Preferences" on page 126.

Adding and Removing New Software Packages

The concept of a software package makes it simple to manage your OpenLinux system. Every software component that is installed on your system is part of a package. OpenLinux includes package management tools to quickly and easily install a new piece of software from the Caldera CD-ROM.

The table beginning on page 190 contains a complete list and brief descriptions of the software packages available on the Caldera CD-ROM.

Software packages on the Caldera CD-ROM are stored in a format called *rpm*. Each rpm file (having a file extension .rpm) contains the files that comprise the software, plus additional information about where to install each file, how much disk space the software requires, and how to run any initialization files that the software provides.

You must be logged in as root to manage software packages. After logging in using your regular username and password, use the su command and the root password to gain superuser access before using the rpm utility.

System administrators may wish to use the glint utility to manage software packages. The glint utility is a graphical package management tool that is located in the Admin Tools group on your Desktop.

If you prefer to use command line utilities, the rpm command can be used. Once you know the location of a package, you can install it with a single command. Packages on the Caldera CD-ROM are located in the / packages directory. For example, to install the XFree86 video driver for SVGA, the command might be as follows (depending on where your CD-ROM is mounted):

```
rpm -i /mnt/cdrom/col/packages/XFree86-SVGA-
3.2.rpm
```

The -i option indicates to install the named package.

If you discover you have installed a package that you don't need any longer, you might first query to make certain it is installed and see how large it is:

```
rpm -qi ispell
```

The -qi option indicates that this is a query, and that you want basic package information for the ispell spell checking package. No path is used, because you are referring to a package that is already installed. The rpm utility knows where to find it.

If you decide to remove this package from your system, based on the information in the query response, you can do so with a single command, using the -u option to uninstall the package.

```
rpm -e ispell
```

You can see a complete list of options and learn more about the rpm command by entering one of these commands:

```
rpm --help
man rpm
```

Working With Users and Groups

Because OpenLinux is a multiuser, multitasking environment, a single computer running OpenLinux may have many users connected at the same time, via various network connections.

The procedures in this section will guide you in some basic user and group account management tasks. These tasks are completed using the graphical User and Groups Configuration tool, usrcfg. If you log in as root before starting the Desktop, these tools appear on the Desktop, ready for you to use. You cannot complete the tasks in this section unless you are logged in as root, because no other user has access permission to change the user and group information files (*/etc/passwd* and */etc/group*).

This is the user configuration dialog used in this section:

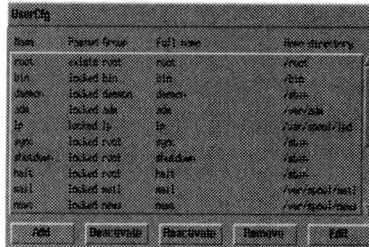

With this tool you can add and remove users and groups, set login shells, full names, home directories, user ids (uids), group ids (gids), etc.

Adding a User

Use this procedure to create a new user account on your system.

1. **Start the graphical User Configuration utility by double-clicking it on the Desktop.**

    If you do not have an icon for the User Configuration utility on your Desktop, you can enter the following command within a graphical terminal emulator window (such as xterm):

    ```
    usercfg
    ```

2. **Choose the Add button in the main window (shown above).**

    A dialog opens with a template for a user.

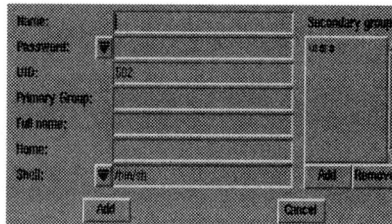

3. **Click in the Username field and enter a username.**

    This is not the user's first and last name; it is the account name that they will use to log in to the system.

    The username cannot include any spaces or punctuation.

    When you complete this field, several other fields will be filled in with default values. You do not need to change any of these default values.

4. **Enter the user's full name.**

5. **Enter a password for this user account in the "Password" field. Confirm it by entering it a second time.**

    You see an asterisk for each character you enter in the Password field.

    You can choose the None option under Password if you are not concerned about security; however, this is not advised.

    If you choose the Lock Password option, this user account cannot be logged in to, except by root using the su command. To restore use of this account, root must adds a password to the account (using this utility, or the passwd command line utility).

6. **Choose OK to complete the password entry.**

7. **Select a login shell using the drop-down menu.**

8. **Choose the Edit option.**

9. **Choose Add to add this user account to the system.**

10. **Choose Yes to create a home directory for this user.**

    If you have already defined a home directory this step will not apply.

    If you will be mounting home directories from another system that is not available at the moment, you should choose No for this step.

Removing a User

1. **Start the graphical User Configuration utility by choosing it on the Desktop.**

If you do not have an icon for the User Configuration utility on your Desktop, you can enter the following command within a graphical terminal emulator window (such as xterm):

```
usercfg
```

2. **Select a user in the main window by clicking on a line.**

3. **Choose the Remove button.**

4. **Confirm that you want to remove this user account from the system.**

5. **Confirm that you want to remove the user's home directory and email information.**

6. **If you are concerned that the user you just removed might still have files on the system, answer Yes to the confirm that you wish to have owner of orphaned files modified.**

   The search and modifications proceed in the background.

   Orphaned files are files which are owned by a name that is not a valid user. If you choose Yes for this step, all orphaned files will have their owner changed to user nobody. You can locate all of these files by using this command in a terminal window:

   ```
   find / ( -group nobody -o -user nobody ) -print
   ```

You may wish to deactivate a user account without removing it. For example, if a user of your system were on an extended vacation, or had not paid for current access to your system, you could temporarily deactivate the user's account.

When a user's account is deactivated, the user cannot log in or access the system, but the user's files are kept intact, waiting for eventual reactivation. The deactivation process is the same as using the Lock option when setting a password for a new user account (see the procedure "Adding a User" on page 66).

When a user returns (or pays the bills), you can quickly re-instate that user's account with the Reactivate procedure below.

Deactivating a User

1. Start the graphical User Configuration utility by choosing it on the Desktop.

    If you do not have an icon for the User Configuration utility on your Desktop, you can enter the following command within a graphical terminal emulator window (such as xterm):

    ```
    usercfg
    ```

2. Select a user in the main window by clicking on a line.

3. Choose the Deactivate button.

4. If you wish to save space while this user is deactivated, choose Yes to compress the user's home directory.

    The gzip and tar commands are used to compress the user's home directory.

Reactivating a User

1. Start the graphical User Configuration utility by choosing it on the Desktop.

    If you do not have an icon for the User Configuration utility on your Desktop, you can enter the following command within a graphical terminal emulator window (such as xterm):

    ```
    usercfg
    ```

2. Select a deactivated user in the main window by clicking on a line.

3. Choose the Reactivate button.

    If the user's home directory was compressed when the user was deactivated, the directory is automatically uncompressed, leaving it as it was previous to deactivation.

In addition to multiple user accounts, OpenLinux can operate with groups of users. Groups are collections of zero or more user accounts. Groups make it more convenient to assign permission to areas of your file system. Several special groups are created automatically during installation.

The group list dialog is shown here:

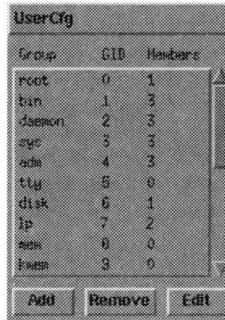

Creating a New Group

1. Start the graphical User Configuration utility by choosing it on the Desk-
    top.

    If you do not have an icon for the User Configuration utility on your
    Desktop, you can enter the following command within a graphical ter-
    minal emulator window (such as xterm):

    ```
    usercfg
    ```

2. Select the Edit Groups item from the UserCfg menu.

3. Choose the Add button.

    A dialog appears where you can enter information for the new group.

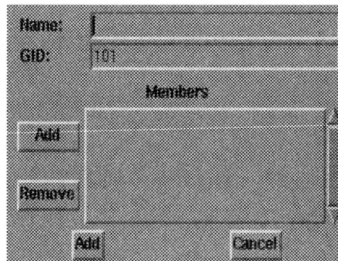

4. Enter a name for the new group.

As with a username, a group name cannot contain spaces or punctuation.

5. **Add members to this new group by choosing the Add button on the left side of the dialog.**

6. **Select users from the list of usernames that appears.**

   Use the Remove button if you make a mistake while adding users.

7. **Choose the Add button on the bottom of the dialog to add this new group to your system.**

   The dialog closes and the new group appears in the list of groups.

Searching Help Systems

The help tool allows you to search man pages, info pages, and plain text document files (or any subset of these) for a regular expression. Search hits are listed and you can double click on them to view them. This tool is very basic, and will be improved over time.

This help tool is most useful for finding information about the Linux operating system, or related features. For information about the Desktop environment, choose the README or Caldera_Info icons on the Desktop. A graphical browser appears from which you can select topics of interest. This browser can also connect you to the Caldera technical information systems via your Internet connection.

Searching in the Linux Help Files

1. **Start the graphical Help Search utility by choosing it on the Desktop.**

   If you do not have an icon for the Help Search utility on your Desktop, you can enter the following command within a graphical terminal emulator window (such as xterm):

   ```
   helptool
   ```

2. **Enter words to search for.**

3. **Choose the Search button to begin the search.**

    After several moments, a list of matching topics appears in the listbox.

4. **Choose a topic to read about by double-clicking on that topic.**

    NOTE

    The Linux Help Files are not integrated at this time with the online help for the Desktop interface. You can view the Desktop online help with the Caldera_Info icon on the Desktop. Choose the "Desktop Overview" option.

Setting Up Initialization Files

The file */etc/rc.d/rc.local* is executed at boot time, after all other initialization is complete. You can add additional initialization commands to this file. For instance, you may want to start up additional daemons, or initialize a printer or some serial ports.

Individual users can have start-up information stored in the hidden file .bash-profile in their home directory. Commands in this file are executed after all system-wide initialization is completed.

CHAPTER 5

Learning to Use the Desktop

The Desktop is a graphical user interface to the Caldera OpenLinux operating system. You can use the Desktop to organize your personal workspace so that the programs, files, and directories you use most often are readily accessible.

With the Desktop, you can run an application (like a spreadsheet or word processor) by double-clicking the program's icon *or* one of its data files.

To move a file between directories, you can drag it from one window to another with the mouse. You can perform tasks such as creating links and changing file ownership and access permissions without typing a single command.

The Desktop interface is included with the CD-ROM in this book, but only as a time-limited test version. The rest of the OpenLinux system will continue to function, but the Desktop interface described in this chapter will only be available for the first 30 days after you install your system.

Following are a few of the tasks that the Desktop simplifies for you:

- Running programs
- Opening files for editing
- Printing files
- Viewing the contents of directories
- Creating new directories
- Moving and removing directories
- Moving, copying, and removing files
- Finding directories and files in your system
- Displaying and changing information about directories and files

This chapter describes how to use the Desktop to organize your work. It provides a brief description of the capabilities of the Desktop and how to use them. A more complete reference to using the Desktop is provided online in the *Desktop User's Guide*, which you can access from the Caldera Info icon on your Desktop.

Starting and Using the Desktop

When your system is first installed, the Desktop is configured as the default application of the X Window System graphical environment. This means that when you start the graphical system (as described below), the Desktop starts. When you exit the Desktop, the graphical system exits, returning you to a character-based display.

You can change the default configuration, so that the Desktop does not start automatically. The online Desktop User Guide contains instructions to do this. Using start-up options during the Desktop initialization is described as well. For example, you can have directories opened automatically, the default colors changed, or sound turned off, as the Desktop starts.

A Brief Tour of the Desktop

The Desktop lets you organize your workspace as you want, placing programs, files, and directories you use most often within easy reach.

When you exit, the Desktop remembers how you left your workspace and restores that arrangement the next time you start the Desktop (unless you specify otherwise with the Layouts option).

The Desktop also lets you name and save an unlimited number of layouts, so you can switch easily from one to another.

The following shows the major windows in a typical Desktop workspace:

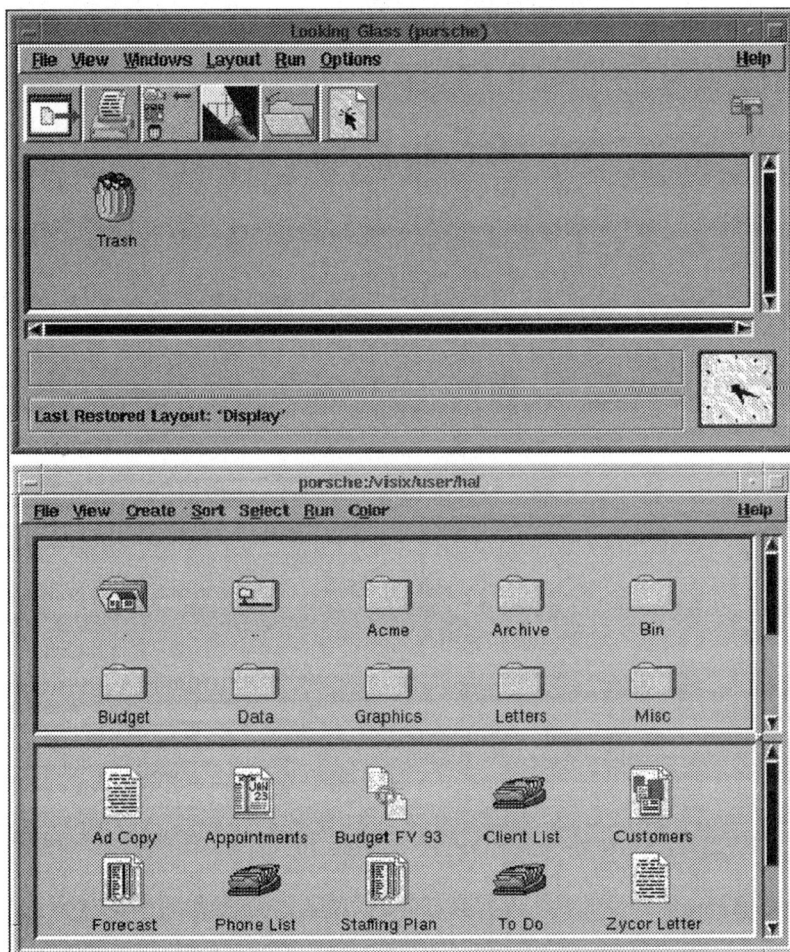

The Desktop Window

The Desktop window is the main window of the Desktop—the background to your other windows. From the Desktop window you can access all Desktop functions. By default, the Desktop window is a full screen display positioned behind all other windows (but you can change this; see the online *Desktop User Guide*).

The Desktop Window

The Desktop window is the main window of the Desktop—the background to your other windows. From the Desktop window you can access all Desktop functions. By default, the Desktop window is a full screen display positioned behind all other windows (but you can change this; see the online *Desktop User Guide*).

The Desktop window includes a large area where you can put frequently-used programs, files, and directories.

Although the objects you put on the Desktop remain in their locations in the file system, they appear on the Desktop for easy access. You can open or activate any object from the Desktop in the same way you can in a directory window.:

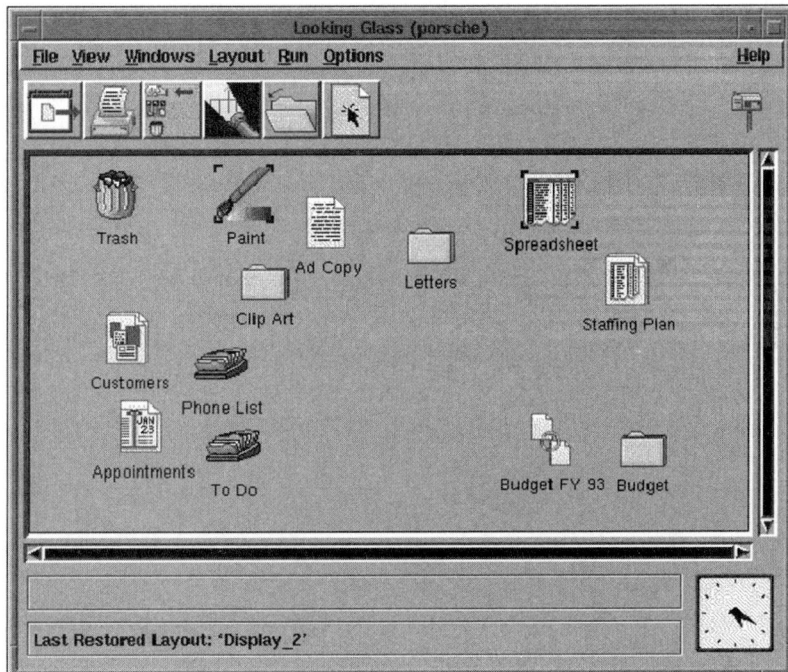

Figure 2:   Desktop window

There are several directory and file icons on the sample Desktop. Objects you put on the Desktop stay there until you take them off.

You might keep directories and files on the Desktop only as needed. For example, you might display the Budget directory when you are working on a budget. Or, if you use your spreadsheet application year-round, you might always keep it on the Desktop.

You can place an object on the Desktop anywhere you want, allowing you to put directories and files in the order most convenient for you.

The icon bar, located beneath the menus in the Desktop window, contains buttons for several Desktop commands and windows. You can add other Desktop commands to the icon bar and create additional buttons to execute external commands.

When you save a workspace layout, the size, position, and contents of the Desktop and icon bar are also saved.

Directory Windows

Directory windows display the contents of a directory. Following is a typical directory window:

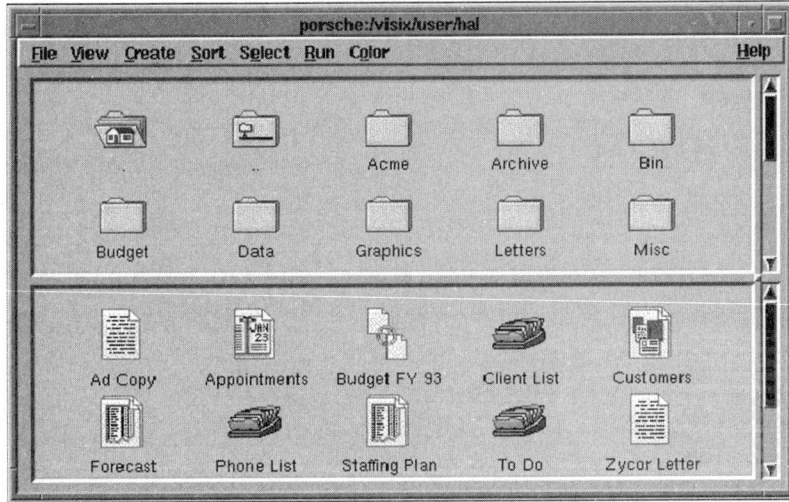

Figure 3:   Sample Directory Window in icon view

From a directory window, you can

- Open and close selected directories and files
- Launch programs
- Change how you view directories and files
- Print files
- Move directories
- Move and copy files
- Remove directories and files

The previous illustration shows a directory window with objects displayed as icons. You can view objects in a directory window by icon, by name, or in a wide format that contains detailed information.

If you have a color monitor, you can also assign colors to object names in directory windows.

Directory windows separate directories from files with a horizontal bar called a *splitter*. The top section displays subdirectories in the directory. The bottom section displays files in the directory.

You can adjust the size of each section by clicking on the splitter and dragging it up or down. You can also remove the splitter and position directories and files anywhere in the directory window.

You can display as many directory windows as you want, but you can only display a directory in one window at a time.

Desktop Icons

Desktop icons represent your directories and files, and can appear in a number of locations. There is an icon for each type of directory or file in your system. The Desktop provides an icon editor for managing icons. With the icon editor, you can

- View the Desktop icons in your system
- Create a personal gallery of icons
- Create new icons
- Edit existing icons

Some characteristics are represented in more than one icon design that comes with the Desktop. Icons with the same design make up an icon family.

Icons with one fold in the upper right corner represent data files that can be opened by more than one application. An example of this type of file is a file that contains only text.

This type of file can be edited by more than one editor or word processor. Icons in this family often contain another visual cue that indicates which application created them, or the type of data in them. Following are examples of icons that represent data files:

Figure 4:   Icon examples, several - data files with one fold.

Icons with two folds in the upper right corner are data files that contain data in a format that is probably meaningful only to the application that created them. Files in this family include the data files that programs create to store your work. Following are examples of icons that represent data files containing data formatted for a specific program:

Figure 5:   Icon examples, several - data files with two folds

The folder icon represents a directory. Within this family are different types of directories. For example, the picture of a house on a folder represents your home directory. The icons for some special directories, however, do not look like folders; NetWare containers, for example. When a directory is open somewhere on your workspace, its folder icon is fanned to make it appear open. Following are examples of icons that represent directories:

Figure 6:   Icon examples, show several - open, closed, home dir

As you work with the Desktop, you will notice other characteristics common to icon families. You can even create some icons with the icon editor. You can access the icon editor from the Run menu on the

Desktop. Instructions for using the Icon Editor are provided in the online *Desktop User Guide*.

Interacting with the Desktop

To use the Desktop, you must already know how to perform a basic set of actions, including

- Selecting items on the desktop and in menus by clicking on them with a mouse or other pointing device
- Selecting buttons and checkboxes by clicking on them
- Dragging and dropping

Most Desktop actions are designed for mouse-based operation, but all Desktop features are also accessible from the keyboard.

Using a Mouse

The following table describes how to use a two-button mouse.

TABLE 4. *Mouse behaviors for a two-button mouse.*

Action	Button
Select and drag items; open a menu	left
Switch between selections	Ctrl+left
Extend selection	Shift+left
Drag selection	both
Drag selection to copy	Ctrl+both
Drag selection to move	Shift+both
Display a pop-up menu of available actions for an item	right

Interacting with Windows and Dialogs

Many windows and dialogs in the Desktop provide several common actions from which users select. The following lists describe actions likely to occur in windows and dialogs. These actions appear in approximately this order in windows. The actions and meanings are

- "Yes" and "No" answer a question and close the window.
- "OK" applies changes you make and closes the window.
- "Apply" applies changes you make but does not close the window.
- "Reset" cancels changes not saved or applied, and does not close the window.
- "Cancel" closes the window without performing actions not already saved or applied to the application.
- "Close" closes the window without performing any action.
- "Help" provides information about the dialog.
- "Stop" ends the current task at the earliest possible breaking point.

Using Accelerator Keys

The Desktop is controlled primarily with a mouse. However, you can also use a key or key combination to perform Desktop operations. In most windows, you can hold down the <Alt> key and press the underlined letter in a menu to select that menu option.

An *accelerator key* is a single key (such as F1) or a key combination (such as Ctrl+Y) assigned to a command in a menu. Using an accelerator key has the same effect as selecting the command from the menu with the mouse.

Many commands can be selected with accelerator keys. If so, the key sequence is displayed at the right of the command in the menu. Accelerator keys are abbreviated in menus. For example, when you see ^Y in the Windows menu in the Desktop window, hold down the Control key and press Y.

A list of accelerator keys is included in the online *Desktop User Guide.*

Introduction to OpenLinux   **83**

Following is an example of a menu with commands and keyboard equivalents:

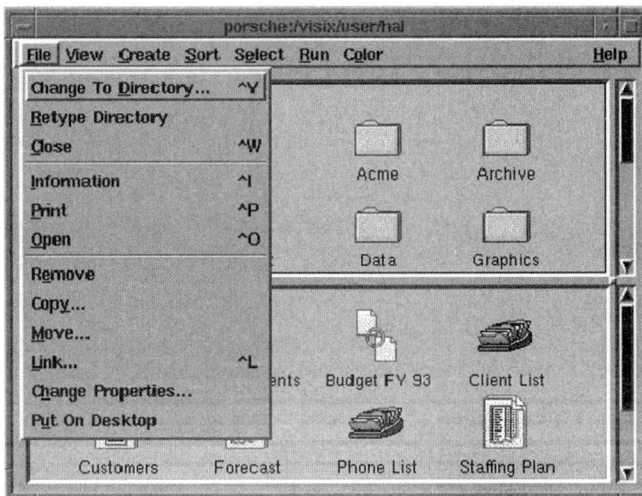

Figure 7:   Menu with command and keyboard equivalents

Working with Directory Windows

To manage your filesystems from the Desktop, you use Directory windows. In Directory windows, you can complete any of these basic operations:

- Opening directories in new directory windows
- Closing directory windows
- Changing the directory displayed in the current directory window
- Moving a directory window to the foreground
- Placing a directory window on the Desktop
- Stacking directory windows

You can also customize the display, including

- Setting display formats for directories
- Sorting directories by name, modification time, or file type

When using the Desktop, there is no single current directory. The *current directory* in each directory window is the directory whose contents are displayed in the window. By default, the full pathname of this directory appears in the title bar of each window.

As part of your display preferences, you can choose the information you want to display in the window's title bar.

In the directory section of each directory window, the current directory is represented by "." (dot). The directory that contains the current directory in each directory window is called the *parent directory*. In the directory section of a directory window, the parent directory is represented by ".." (dot dot).

The following example shows current and parent directories in a directory window:

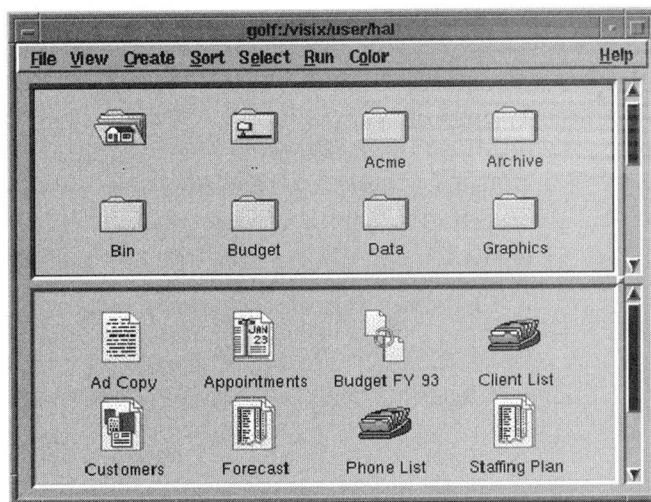

Figure 8:   Current and parent directories in a directory window

The first time you open a directory window, your default display preferences determine what the window looks like. You can then use the File, View, Sort, and Color menus in the directory window to set the display, such as

- Which directory appears
- Whether directories and files are displayed in Name, Icon, or Wide view
- Whether the directory window contains the splitter or is in position-able format
- The order that directories and files appear in a split window
- The colors of objects in Name, Icon, or Wide view

The Desktop remembers a directory window's display settings and position on your workspace the next time you open the window.

Opening Directory Windows

The first time you start the Desktop, no directory windows are open. There are several ways to open directory windows to start working with your files and directories:

- Use the Windows | Open Directory command on the Desktop. Enter a directory path in the Open Directory dialog, or choose one from the History List shown.
- Select a directory in a directory window and use the File | Open command in its directory window.
- Select a directory or file on your Desktop and click the Show In Directory Window button on the icon bar.
- Double-click any directory you want to open in a directory window.
- Click the Open Directory Window button on the icon bar.

The Open Directory window looks like this:

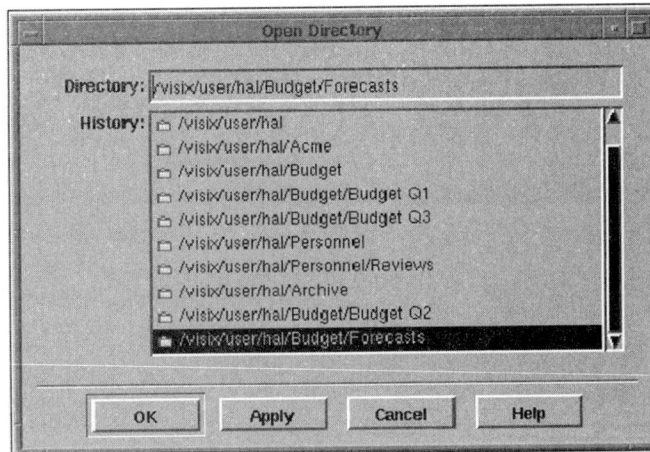

Figure 9: The Open Directory Window

Closing Directory Windows

Any directory window can be closed by choosing File | Close in that directory window.

Moving Directory Windows

If you have several directory windows open, there are several ways you can arrange the directory windows:

- Use the Windows menu in the Desktop window to move a window to the front (choosing it by name).
- You can also use the Windows menu or the Stack Directory Windows button on the icon bar to stack all directory windows neatly on the workspace.
- You can hold down the <Alt> key and press the <Tab> key to switch between all open desktop windows, including all directory windows.

Directory Window Views

You can view directories and files in directory windows in the any of three views by selecting one of the following items from the View menu in a directory window:

- Name
- Icon
- Wide

Name View. When directories and files are displayed in Name view, a miniature icon next to each name indicates whether the object is a directory or file. For example,

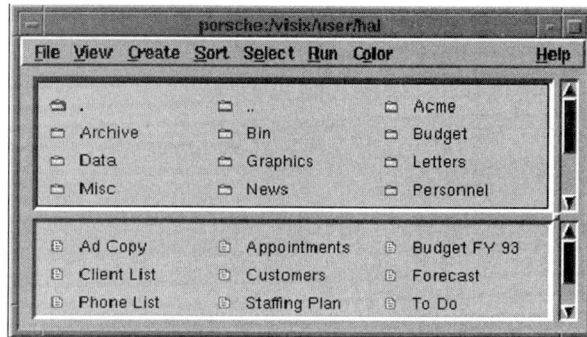

Figure 10: Hals home directory displayed by name.

Icon View. When directories and files are displayed in Icon view, a full-size icon appears for each object. The icon is selected based on file-typing rules used by the Desktop. The name appears below the icon. For example,

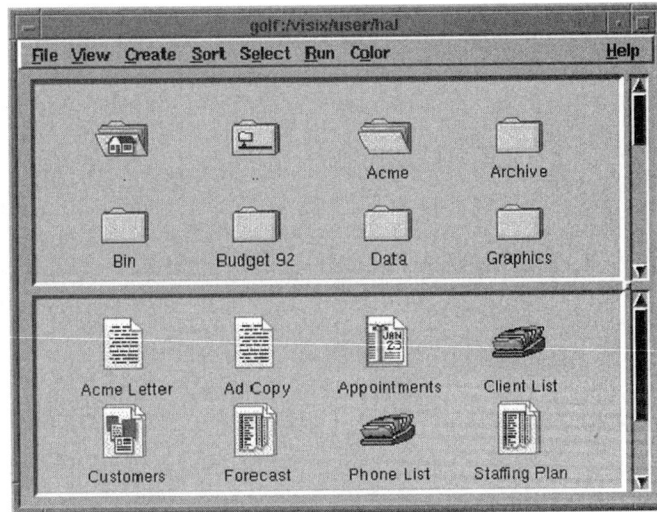

Figure 11: Hals home directory displayed by icon.

Wide View. When directories and files are displayed in Wide view, the following information can be displayed in any order:

- Name
- Access privileges
- Owner and Group
- Number of links
- Size (in bytes)
- Inode number
- Time and date of last update
- File type
- Link content

A miniature icon next to each name indicates whether the object is a directory or file.

The following is an example of directories and files displayed in Wide view:

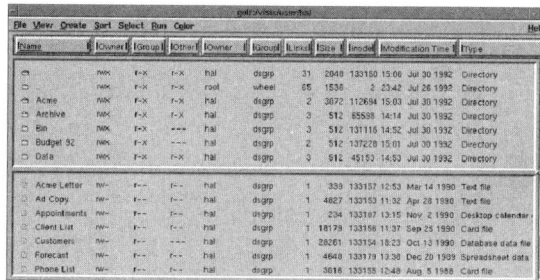

Figure 12: Hals directories and files displayed in Wide view

You might need to resize a directory window or adjust the size or position of column headings to see the information you want in Wide view. This information is saved and displayed the next time you open this window.

The following table describes actions you can use to adjust the display of information in Wide view.

TABLE 5. *Adjusting the display of information in Wide view.*

To	Do this
Increase or decrease the width of a column	Drag the handle on either edge of the column heading to the left or right
Move a column from one position to another	Drag the column heading to a new position on the title line
Remove a category from the display	Drag the column heading down off of the title line. The name cannot be removed.
Eliminate unused space between all categories	Double-click in the gray area between headings in the title line.
Sort by category	Double-click a column heading.

To change default views for Desktop directory windows, see "Changing Display Preferences" on page 136.

Sorting Directories and Files

You can sort directories and files in a directory window according to a specific category and in a particular order.

When directories and files are displayed in Icon or Name view in a positionable directory window, you can sort by the following categories, in ascending or descending order:

- Directory or file name
- Color (of an icon's text)
- Type

When directories and files are displayed in Wide view, you can sort by the following categories, in ascending or descending order:

- File or directory name
- Color (of an icon's text)
- Owner name
- Group name
- Size
- Time and date the directory or file was last changed
- File type

To sort by a displayed category in Wide view, double-click a column heading. (If a category has been removed from the Wide view display, you cannot sort by that category; use the View menu to show the category again.)

Sorting by Category

1. **In a directory window, from the Sort menu, choose a sorting category.**

    The directories and files in the current directory window are sorted and redisplayed.

    To change the sort order, in a directory window choose Sort | Ascending or Sort | Descending. Your choice appears selected in the menu and a filled-in square appears in front of the command in the Sort menu.

If you sort by color, the ascending sort order is shown in the Color menu in a directory window: black items are first, followed by brown, green, blue, purple, pink, red, and orange. Objects that are the same color sort alphabetically.

Retyping a Directory

When the Desktop first accesses a directory, it looks at the directories and files to determine their *type*, based on the rules defined for your system or site. This information is stored in a hidden file to improve performance.

When the Desktop accesses a directory it has been in, it only examines files added since its last visit. However, if you execute a file, it is examined again, as a security measure.

Correctly determining a file type is very important because the Desktop uses the information in several ways, including

- To display the correct icon when files are viewed by icon
- To carry out the correct action when files are activated
- To determine whether files are printable and to print them correctly
- To determine whether a program must be run in a terminal emulator window

If you add a new rule (using the right mouse menu), the Desktop automatically *retypes* the directory. If you experience problems with file types, the Desktop has an option for retyping directories.

1. **Open a directory window for the directory you want to retype.**

2. **Choose File | Retype Directory.**

    The directory is retyped.

Managing Directories and Files

In this section, you learn how to

- Create directories and files
- Create links for directories and files
- Find and display directories and files in directory windows
- Select directories and files in the active directory window
- Group selected directories and files
- Move directories
- Move and copy files
- Remove directories and files
- Print files

Creating Directories and Files

Use the Create menu in a directory window to create directories, files, FIFOs, and devices. (FIFOs and devices are like files but are used to communicate between programs or with peripheral devices.)

1. **In a directory window, choose the Create menu, followed by the type of object you want to create.**

2. **Type a new name for the object while it is selected.**

   If you are creating a device, you must enter major and minor device numbers. Devices are usually created only by system administrators. This should not be needed on your Caldera system.

Changing the Name of an Existing Directory or File

1. **Select the name of the directory or file you want to change in a directory window.**

   A box appears around the directory or file name and the name is highlighted.

2. **Edit the name as you would a text field.**

   You can change the name of all directories and files in your directory except the "." (current) and ".." (parent) directories.

   If you make a mistake, delete the entire name and press Enter. The old name is restored.

Creating Links

A link lets you access a directory or file from more than one location in a file system or directory hierarchy.

You use a different type of link depending on how you want to reference a directory or file. Symbolic links take up little disk space—much less than a copy of the directory or file. You can view or make changes to a file or directory through a link.

You can create two types of links:

- Hard
- Symbolic

A *hard link* is a reference to a physical file; a *symbolic link* is a reference to a directory or file name.

You can only create Hard links for files, not for directories. The link can be in a different directory but it must be on the same file system. A file is not removed from your system until all its hard link names are removed.

To find out how many hard links a file has, in the file's directory window choose File | Information, or choose Wide View (links are shown in the Links column).

Unlike a hard link, a symbolic link can be made across file systems and can reference directories and files. When you create a symbolic link, a file is created that contains the pathname of the actual directory or file. As with a hard link, you can view or make changes to a file through its symbolic links.

Because a symbolic link only points to a directory or file name and is not an actual file system reference, when you remove the original directory or file you also make all its symbolic links invalid.

The link is still there, but because it points to nothing, the link causes errors if you try to use it. The symbolic link becomes available again if you put a file with the same name in the same location.

There are two types of symbolic links:

- Absolute
- Relative

An *absolute symbolic link* is a full pathname that leads to the original directory or file. Because it explicitly refers to each directory in the pathname, you create an absolute symbolic link if you keep the original directory or file in the same location in the directory structure.

However, you can move the linked reference, because its location does not determine the reference. If you remove, move, or change the name of the original directory or file, you cannot access that directory or file because the pathname is invalid.

A *relative symbolic link* is a relative pathname that leads to the original directory or file. The location of the linked reference is used to determine the location of the original directory or file, so one cannot move relative to the other without making the link invalid.

Relative symbolic links let you move the portion of the directory structure containing the original directory or file and the linked reference within the file system. (For more about the types of links supported by your system, see the online Linux system documentation.)

Creating a Link

1. Select the files you want to create a link for.

2. In the directory window, choose File | Link.

The Link Files and Directories window appears:

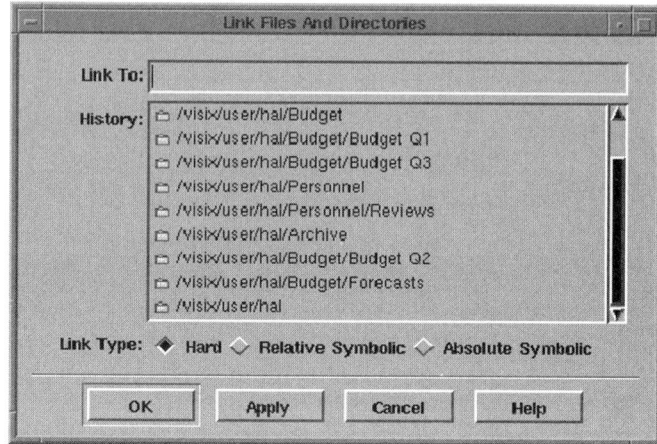

Figure 13: Link window with Hard link button pressed

3.   **Specify where the linked reference will appear and its name by doing one of the following:**

   • From the history list, select the directory you want the linked reference to appear in.

   • In the Link To field, enter the full or relative pathname of the directory you want the link to appear in, or enter the full or relative pathname of the link.

   • Clear the Link To field and press Enter to create the link in your home directory.

   The Link To field also supports directory name completion. If you type a partial name of a directory that is unique and then press the spacebar, that directory name is completed in the Link To field.

   If you select more than one file in step 1, you can only specify a directory path, not a file name.

4.   **Select the type of link you want to create.**

   If you try to create a link having the same name as a file that exists in the directory you want to put a hard link in, a message appears asking if you want to overwrite the file.

(If the Relative Symbolic and Absolute Symbolic buttons do not appear in the Link Files and Directories window, you are viewing a file system that does not support symbolic links—for example, an automounted NetWare volume.)

5. **Choose one of the following:**

   - To save changes and exit the Link Files and Directories window, click OK.
   - To save changes without closing the window, click Apply.

   The link is created in the directory you chose.

   If you create links for several directories or files at one time, a status dialog appears, allowing you to cancel the unfinished part of the operation by clicking Cancel.

   You can set the access permissions for symbolic links but not for hard links. (To set access permissions, see "Changing Access Permissions" on page 104.)

Finding Directories and Files

Use the Find command to search your file system for a specific directory or file. The Find command is available from two menus in the Desktop:

- The Windows menu in the Desktop window
- The Select menu in a directory window

In the Find window, you specify a name or a pattern (using special characters) that you want the Desktop to search for. The Desktop lists the names of matching directories and files in the scrolling list. The following shows the Find window:

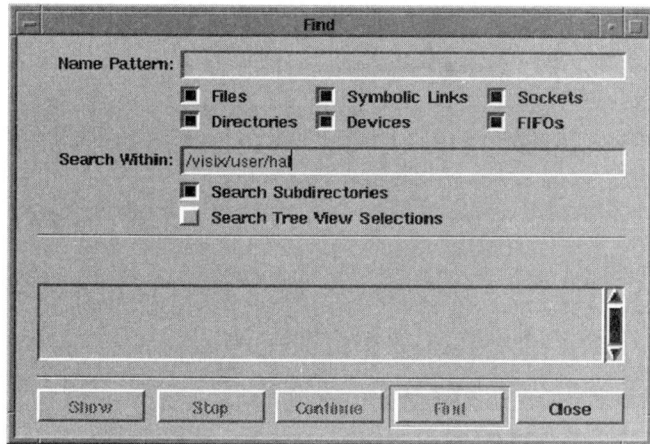

Figure 14: Find window

From the list of matching directories and files, you can select a directory or file and click Find | Show to display it in a directory window.

When you use Find to search for a file or directory, you enter a pattern that the Desktop matches for you. The following table describes special characters you can use in the search pattern.

TABLE 6. *Special characters used in a pattern for the Find Window*

To specify a pattern that includes	Use this character
A single, variable character.	?
For example, memo? finds all names that begin with memo followed by exactly one character (like memo1 or memoX, but not memo, memo10, or memoXY).	

TABLE 6. *Special characters used in a pattern for the Find Window*

To specify a pattern that includes	Use this character
One character from a set of characters.	[ ]
For example, Wor[dkm] finds names that begin with Wor and end in d, k, or m (Word, Work, Worm).	
Zero or more variable characters.	*
For example, *.c finds names with the .c extension (Paper.c, PROG.c, Classworkprog.c).	

Moving and Copying Files and Directories

In the Desktop, you can move and copy files and directories by using mouse actions or the File Move or File | Copy command.

You can move or copy a file or directory from one directory to another in two ways:

- Drag the file or directory to its new location

  If you want to copy a file or directory instead of moving it, hold down the <Ctrl> key when you click and drag the icon.

- Select the file or directory and choose the File | Move command

Removing Directories and Files

In the Desktop, you can delete directories and files from your system in two ways:

- Select a directory or file and choose the File | Remove command
- Drag a file or directory to the Trashcan icon

Depending on how you set your preferences, when you use the File | Remove command to remove a file, it might be permanently deleted. When you remove a directory, the directory and all its files and subdirectories might also be permanently deleted.

When you remove a file by dragging it to the Trashcan, it might be stored there until you "Empty" the Trashcan. If you decide you need the file, you can retrieve it from the Trashcan before you empty it.

Your removal preferences are described in "Changing Removal Preferences" on page 138. If you accidentally remove something, see your system administrator—it might be recoverable from a backup.

The Trash Window

Use the Trash window to view the contents of the trash can, displaying items in Name or Icon view. To see the Trash window, double-click on the Trash icon. The Trash window is shown here:

Figure 15: Trash Window

In the Trash window, you can also

- Show the origin or full pathname of items
- Show the date and time an item was placed in the trash
- Retrieve items
- View an information window for items

Displaying the Original Location of Items in the Trash

1. In the Trash window, select an item or items.

2. Select File | Show Origin to view the full pathname of the item's origin.

The Origin window appears:

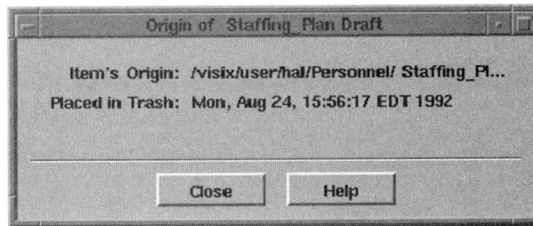

Figure 16: Origin Window

3. (Optional) To open an information window for the item, select File | Information.

Printing Files

You can print files on the Desktop or from a directory window by selecting a file and choosing the File | Print command. If you try to print a file that is not printable, the Desktop displays a dialog telling you it will not be printed.

When the Desktop prints a file, it uses two commands: one to format the file and one to spool it to the printer. Files printed to NetWare Print Queues use a different system, however.

You can specify the print formatter and spooler commands as part of your execution preferences. (See "Changing Execution Preferences" on page 130.) The formatter command processes the file for printing. For example, it might paginate the document or put in headers. The spooler receives the data produced by the formatter command and sends it to the printer.

When you choose File | Print, the Desktop checks to see if the file is printable. If it is, the Desktop checks to see if a special formatting command is defined for that type of file. If there is, the Desktop uses it. If not, the Desktop uses the command from the user's execution preferences.

The output of the formatting step is then sent to the spooler command specified in the user's execution preferences.

Viewing and Changing Directory and File Attributes

You can use the Information command in a directory window to open a window that contains information about a directory or file, including

- Name
- Type
- Size (in bytes)
- Number of links to the directory or file
- Inode number (a number used by the operating system to identify the file)
- Access permissions (also called *protection mode*)
- Ownership and group reference
- Date and time the directory or file was created or modified
- Date and time the status of the directory or file was changed
- Date and time the directory or file was last accessed or changed
- Link information (symbolic links only)
- Referenced protection (symbolic links only)
- Device type (devices only)
- Major and minor device numbers (devices only)

You can also change the following using the information window:

- Name
- Access permissions
- Ownership and group reference
- Date and time the directory or file was last accessed or changed
- Link information (symbolic links only)

- Referenced protection (symbolic links only)
- Device type (devices only)
- Major and minor device numbers (devices only)

Viewing Directory or File Information

1. **In a directory window, select the directories and files you want to view information for.**

2. **Choose File | Information.**

    An information window appears for each directory and file.

    The window is divided into sections: The first contains information about the directory or file; the second contains radio buttons that control information shown in the third section about the selected directory or file:

    - The Access button, which displays access permissions (the default).
    - The Ownership button, which displays owner, group reference, and ID.
    - The Dates button, which displays status change, access, and modification dates.
    - If you are viewing a device file, the Device button, which displays information about devices.

Following is an example of an information window:

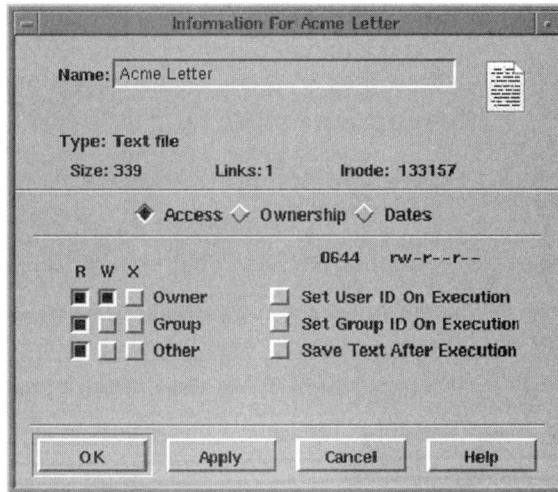

3. Click the appropriate button in the second section to view a different category of information in the third section of the window.

4. When you finish viewing the information, click OK to save changes and close the information window, or click Apply to save changes without closing the window.

Changing Access Permissions

You can change access permissions for any directory or file you own. You can grant access permissions to yourself as the owner, to members of your group, and to others (users not in your group).

The following summarizes the access permissions you can assign.

TABLE 7. *Directory and file access permissions*

If you assign this permission	For a directory, specified users can	For a file, specified users can
R (read)	View its contents	View its contents
W (write)	Put directories or files in it & remove directories or files from it	Change its contents
X (execute)	Search the directory	Run it as a command

Only assign the execute permission for files used as commands. If you assign execute permission for an ordinary file, someone might try to run it as a command, in which case the system interprets its contents as commands. This can produce unpredictable results.

Changing Access Permissions

1. In a directory window, select the directories and files you want to change access permissions for.

2. Choose File | Information.

   An information window appears for each selected directory and file.

3. Select Access.

The access information appears on the left in the third section as follows:

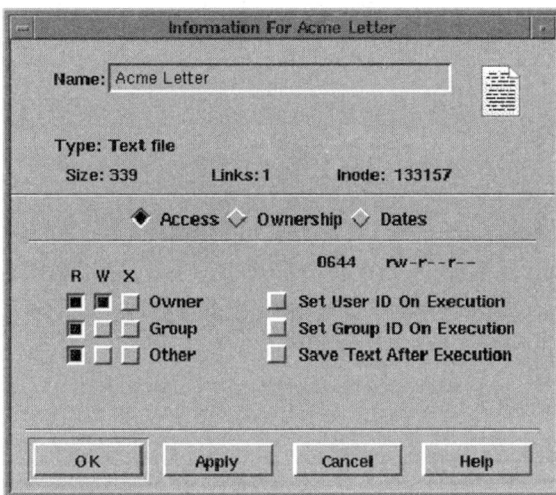

Figure 17: Information window with access information.

If the directory or file is a symbolic link, two buttons appear below the access information: the Link Protection button and the Referenced Protection button.

These buttons let you choose whether to view and set the protection for the link or for the directory or file it references. (For more about links, see "Creating Links" on page 94.)

The Link Protection button is selected by default. With this button selected, you view access permissions for the link, not for the file the link refers to.

To view access information for the actual directory or file (the directory or file a link references), select Referenced Protection.

4. **Select permissions as follows:**

- R (read) to allow the owner, group, or others to view the contents of the directory or file

- W (write) to allow the owner, group, or others to change the contents of a file, or to put files in or remove files from a directory

- X (execute) to allow the owner, group, or others to run a file as a command or open a directory

5. **Click OK to save changes and close the information window, or click Apply to save changes without closing the window.**

    If you selected more than one directory or file, repeat Steps 3 through 5 until all information windows are closed.

Changing Execution Options

In addition to viewing access permissions for a directory or file, you can also view and change execution options. These options include

- The Set User ID On Execution and Set Group ID On Execution options, which allow other users to execute a program with the access permissions of the program's owner or group. Use these permissions with extreme care: they can give other users control over your files.
- The Save Text After Execution option (or *sticky bit*), which causes an executable file to be marked so it is less likely to be swapped out to disk between uses. Use this option with care: it improves the performance of the application, but can affect the performance of more important applications.

Although these options may only seem meaningful for executable files, they can also affect directories on some systems (for more information, see your system administrator).

Changing Ownership and Group Reference

Every directory and file has an owner and a group reference. You are the owner of directories and files you create. If you own a directory or file, you control

- Who owns it
- Which group it is associated with
- Who can view it
- Who can change it
- Who can execute it (if it is a program)

You can only change the ownership of a file or directory if you are the root user. You can only change the group reference of a file or directory if you are a member of the group you are giving ownership to (or if you are the root user).

When you specify the group reference for a directory or file, you identify a group of users that you (or the owner of the directory or file) can specify a separate set of access permissions for.

If you are logged in as the root user to do administrative tasks, you can use the Information command to change directory or file ownership one object at a time.

Changing Ownership and Group Reference

1. In a directory window, select the directories and files you want to change the ownership or group reference for.

2. Choose File | Information.

    An information window appears for each directory and file.

3. Select Ownership.

The ownership and group reference information appears in the third section of the window. The owner list is an alphabetical list of users on your system. The group list is an alphabetical list of groups on your system.

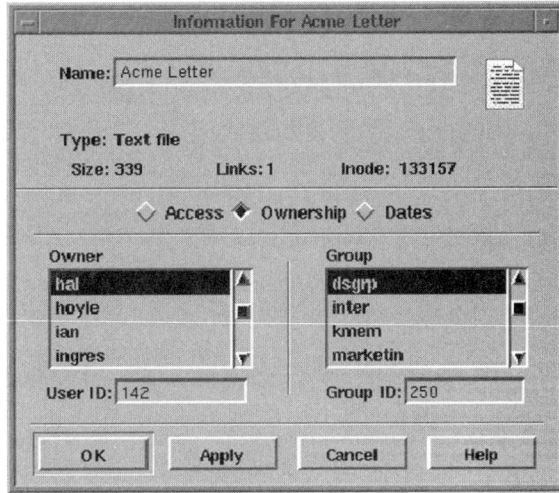

Figure 18: Information window with ownership and group ref information.

4.   **Specify the new owner or group by doing one of the following:**

  •   Select a name from the owner list or select a group from the group list.

  •   Enter the ID number of the owner or group in the text box below the list.

5.   **Click OK to save changes and close the information window, or click Apply to save changes without closing the window.**

If you selected more than one directory or file, repeat Steps 3 through 5 until all information windows are closed.

Changing Information for a Group of Directories and Files

With the Information command, to change information for a group of 20 files or directories, you would have to change the same information in 20 windows.

With the Change Properties command, you can change the following information for a group of selected directories and files in one operation:

- Ownership and group reference
- Access permissions (also called *protection mode*)
- Execution options
- Date and time the directories or files were last modified or accessed

To change information for a group of selected file at the same time, you must be logged in as the root user. Complete the following:

1. In a directory window, select the group of directories and files you want to change ownership or group reference for.

2. Choose File | Change Properties.

   The Change Properties window appears:

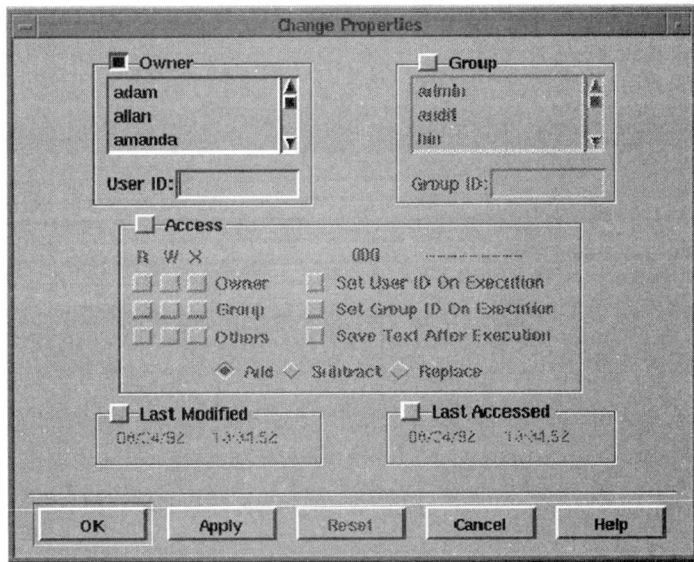

   The window contains several sections and a row of buttons at the bottom. The sections display ownership and group reference information, access permission and execution option information, and date and time information.

3. Select the buttons for the information you want to change.

   When you make a selection, that part of the window becomes active.

4. Specify the new information for the selected directories and files.

5. Choose one:

   • To save changes and close the Change Properties window, click OK.

   • To save changes without closing the window, click Apply.

   • To revert to the last saved values without closing the window, click Revert.

Running Programs

Using the Desktop, you can run and terminate programs from

• Directory windows and the Desktop window

• Terminal emulator windows

In this section you also learn how to

• View available actions for a file

Activating Files

When you activate a file, the Desktop decides what type of file it is and runs the correct program. When the Desktop runs a program, the program's icon and process ID are displayed in the Jobs window, shown below. (To open the Jobs window, select Windows | Jobs in the Desktop window.))

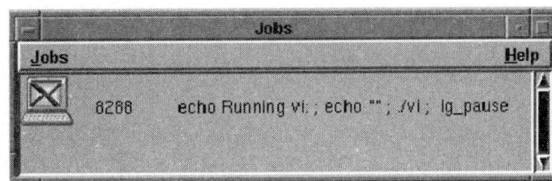

Figure 19: Jobs Window with vi icon

You can usually terminate a program started from the Desktop in the Jobs window by using Jobs | Request Job Termination (preferred) or Jobs | Force Job Termination (when necessary).

There are three ways to activate a file in the Desktop:

- Double-click the file icon

    If actions are associated with the file, the file is activated, and the Desktop displays the icon for the default program associated with the file in the Jobs window. The Desktop notifies you if no actions are associated with a file.

- Select the file and choose the File | Open command

    If actions are associated with the file, the file is activated and the Desktop displays in the Jobs window the icon for the default program associated with the file. The Desktop notifies you if no actions are associated with the file.

- Drag and drop the file onto a *drop receiver.*

    Drop receivers are file types with special rules defined that enable them to run programs when files are dropped onto them. Drop receivers have icons with bold corner brackets. An example of a drop receiver is a word processor: to run the program and edit a document, drag the document icon and drop it onto the word processor icon.

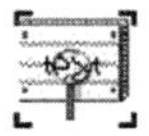

Figure 20: Drop receiver word processor icon with corner
brackets

If no actions for the drop receiver file are associated with the selected file or for one of multiple files, the Desktop displays the Bad Drop cursor, and an X appears on the drop receiver:

Figure 21: Bad drop Icon.

If there are actions for the drop receiver file associated with the selected file or for all files selected, the Desktop displays the Good Drop cursor and highlights the drop receiver.

Figure 22: Good drop icon.

Viewing and Selecting File Actions

Some files have more than one action associated with them. The action that occurs when you double-click a file (or select it and choose File | Open) is called its default action.

The Desktop lets you view all possible actions for a file and activate one. If you are not sure what a file's default action is, view the possible actions before activating it. Selecting an action from the list of possible actions does not change the default action for the file.

Selecting File Actions Using the Pop-up Menu

1. Move the cursor to a file.

2. Press the Menu button on your mouse (usually the right button).

    If actions are associated with the file, the pop-up menu list the actions, with the default action listed first. If no are actions associated with the file, the Edit File Actions option appears as the only menu item.

3. Select the file action you want to run.

Viewing and Selecting File Actions in the File Actions Window

1. From the pop-up menu, select Edit File Actions (or Ctrl+double-click the file).

The File Actions window opens:

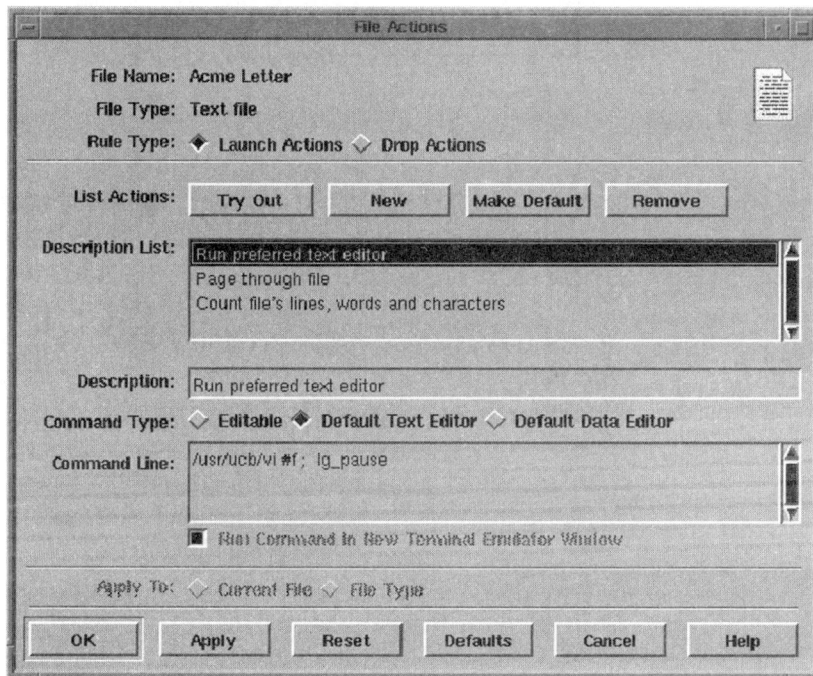

Figure 23: File Actions Window

If no actions are associated with the file, the Description List, Description, and Command Line sections are empty.

If actions are associated with the file, the Description List section contains descriptions of all possible actions, with the default action for the file highlighted and listed first. It is described in the Description section, and the associated command appears in the Command Line section.

2. **In the Description List scrolling list, double-click a file action to run.**

Customizing File Actions

Initial file actions are determined by the system rulebase, which is controlled by the system administrator. However, the Desktop lets you create and edit user-specific file actions for a file or for all files of a specific type.

Use the File Actions window to enter these file actions and save them to your custom rulebase. Customizing file actions for yourself does not affect the system's rulebase. (You can always restore the system rulebase file actions.)

You can use several symbols to define file actions for the Desktop, in addition to those used by your shell. The special Desktop symbols are described in the following table.

TABLE 8. *Values of symbols used in the Command Line window*

This option	Inserts this symbol	With this value
Selected Files	#f	The names of all files selected in the directory window or on the Desktop.
	#F	The full pathnames of selected files.
Selected Directories	#d	The names of all directories selected in the directory window or on the Desktop.
	#D	The full pathnames of selected directories.
Effective User	#u	The current user name.
Effective Group	#g	The group name associated with the Desktop process.
Current Directory	#c	The full pathname of the current directory, or the user's home directory if running from the Desktop window rather than a directory window.
		This current directory appears as the title of the Command Line window.
Drop Receiver	#r	The name of the drop receiver associated with selected files.
	#R	The full pathname of the drop receiver associated with selected files.

Editing File Actions

1. Use the right-click menu on any object to open the Edit File Actions window.

2. Select one of the following rule types:

    *   **Launch Actions** to edit launch actions for a file
    *   **Drop Actions** to edit drop actions for a drop target

3. From the description list, select the file action you want to edit.

4. In the Command Type section, make the appropriate selection.

    All file actions that exist or are created in the custom rulebase are editable except the Default Text Editor and the Default Data Editor.

    If you select Default Text Editor or Default Data Editor (set as Execution Preferences) you cannot edit a file action in the description list.

    If you have not listed text or data editors for file actions, selecting Default Text Editor or Default Data Editor enters the appropriate editor as "preferred" in the description list.

5. In the Description text box, make needed changes to the description of the file action.

6. In the Command Line text box, make needed changes to the command for the file action.

    The contents of this field are passed to the operating system shell when this action is selected.

    Your command can contain any text or symbols allowed by your operating system shell, including environment variables. You can also embed Desktop special symbols. (For a list of Desktop symbols, see the table on page 115.)

7. Select or unselect the Run Command In New Terminal Emulator window checkbox.

    This checkbox is located below the Command Line text box. When activated, it runs the command for a file action in a new terminal window.

8. In the Apply To field, select either Current File or File Type.

This restricts a file action to the selected file only or to all files of the same type (as displayed in the File Type field at the top of the window).

9. **Choose one**

   - To update your custom rulebase and exit File Actions, click **OK**.

   - To save changes without closing the window, click **Apply**.

   - To discard changes made since your custom rulebase was saved, click **Reset**.

   - To reset your rulebase to the system rulebase, click **Defaults**.

   If the rule you delete is a custom rule that applies to a specific file, and a custom rule exists for that file type, the per-file rule is discarded and the custom file type rule applies.

Customizing Your Workspace

This section shows you how to customize your workspace and tools. You learn how to

- Customize the icon bar
- Add and remove directories and files
- View directories and files by name or icon
- View the full pathname of directories and files
- Open directories and files
- Show directories and files on the Desktop in directory windows
- Print files
- Move directories and files around
- Clean up the Desktop
- Use the trash can
- Receive mail notification
- Create external commands
- Create icons for external commands and place them on the icon bar

The Icon Bar

The icon bar is an important feature of the Desktop window. It contains a row of graphic buttons that open various Desktop windows, launch applications, or open command dialogs.

To view the name of a button, hold down the mouse button while pointing to the button. Its name appears in the first text box in the status area at the bottom of the Desktop window. (First, select View | View Status Area.) Click a button to execute the associated action.

Generally, the buttons supplied with the Desktop provide shortcuts for operations that can also be performed using Desktop menu commands. However, you can add buttons to the icon bar that do things not available on a Desktop menu.

The Icon Bar command lets you control the appearance and contents of the icon bar.

When you select Options | Icon Bar in the Desktop window, the Icon Bar window appears:

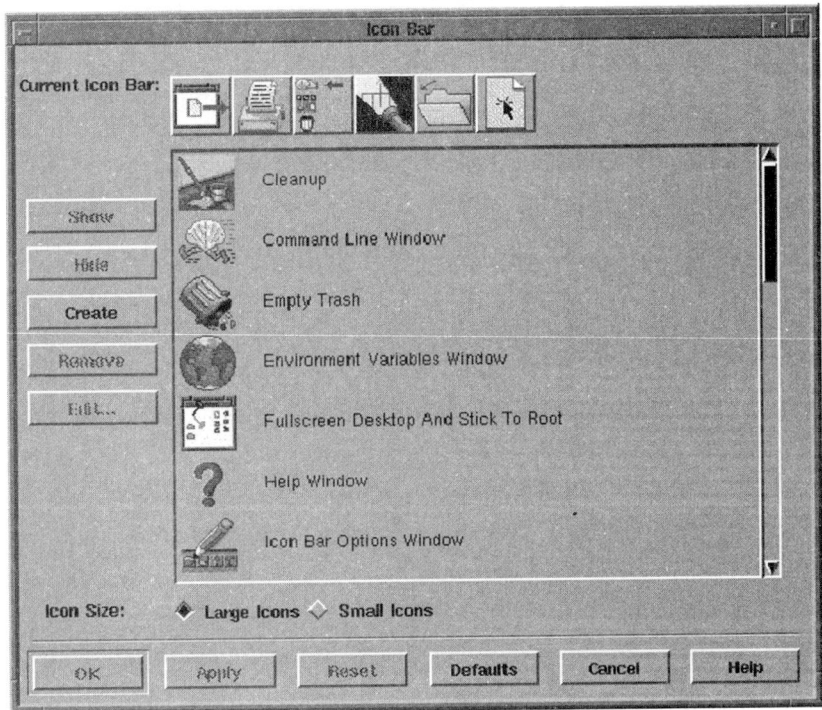

Figure 24: Icon Bar Window

Internal Icon Bar Buttons. The window lists icon bar buttons and custom external buttons you create. Custom buttons you create are listed first, in order of creation, followed by an alphabetical list of internal buttons. You can show internal Desktop buttons on the icon bar, but you cannot edit or remove them from the list. These buttons are

- Cleanup. Aligns icons to an invisible grid
- Command Line Window. Opens a command line window
- Empty Trash. Removes files and directories in the trash can.
- Environment Variables Window. Opens the Environment Variables window.

- Fullscreen Desktop and Stick to Root. Makes the Desktop window fullscreen.
- Help Window. Opens the Help system.
- Icon Bar Window. Opens the window to edit the icon bar.
- Jobs Window. Opens the Jobs window, listing active system processes that were started from the Desktop.
- Layouts Window. Opens the Layouts window, to show and edit custom layouts.
- Open Current Selection. Starts or opens a selected object.
- Open Directory Window. Opens a directory window for a selected object.
- Open Find Window. Opens the Find window to search for an object.
- Preferences Window. Opens the Preferences window to see or edit preferences.
- Print Current Selection. Prints the selected file.
- Run Terminal Emulator. Opens a terminal emulator window (such as xterm).
- Run Icon Editor. Starts the icon editor.
- Show Full Pathname. Switches between showing just filename and full paths.
- Show in Directory Window. Opens a directory window containing a selected object in its parent directory.
- Stack directory windows. Stacks all open directory windows with all title bars visible.
- Take Off Desktop. Removes selected objects from the Desktop (but not the file system).
- Toggle Sound On/Off. Switches sound on or off.
- Toggle Stick Desktop to Root. Switches the Desktop between being fullscreen and sizeable (non-fullscreen).

Five buttons at the left of the list perform various actions. Depending on the item selected in the scrolling list, some of the following buttons might appear dimmed when you first open the icon bar window:

- **Show.** Use to add a button to the icon bar. If an item is on the icon bar, a mark appears next to its name in the list and Show is disabled.
- **Hide.** Use to take a button off the icon bar. If an icon is not on the icon bar, Hide is disabled.
- **Create.** Use to create a button and an associated external command (see "Customizing the Icon Bar with New External Commands" on page 121).
- **Remove.** Use to discard a button you created.
- **Edit.** Use to edit a button you created.

If you show many icons on the icon bar, or if you unstick the Desktop from the root and resize it, there might not be sufficient room to display all icons on the icon bar.

Customizing the Icon Bar with New External Commands. In the icon bar window you can create external commands and associate them with buttons you design. You can show the buttons on the icon bar for easy access.

You can define a command and create an icon for the command button in the same procedure, but you might want to perform these steps separately.

You can also define the command and use a generic Desktop icon for its button and specify a custom button later.

To create a new external command, click Create. Double-click on the new icon that appears, and fill in the fields of the Edit External window:

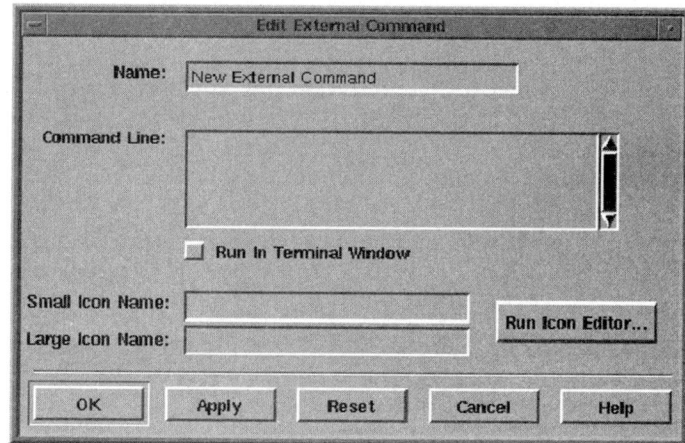

Figure 25: Edit External Command.

Directories and Files on the Desktop

There are two ways to put a directory or file from a directory window on the Desktop:

- Drag the directory or file to the Desktop
- Use the Put On Desktop command

You can remove a directory or file from the Desktop by selecting the directory or file you want to remove, and choosing File | Take Off Desktop.

When you remove a directory or file from the Desktop, the directory or file no longer appears on the Desktop. It still exists in its original location in the file system. Taking an object off the Desktop is not the same as removing an object with File | Remove or dragging it to the trash can.

Working with Layouts

You can arrange your workspace in many ways and then name and save each arrangement as a *layout*.

A layout is a specific arrangement of a workspace and includes the appearance and contents of the Desktop window and any other open Desktop windows (except preferences windows). Saving a layout makes it easy to switch from one activity to another without manually rearranging the windows.

For example, you could save a layout for working on budgets that would include your spreadsheet program, documents you are working on, and a directory icon representing the directory in which you keep business plans. Ordinarily, when the Desktop starts, it restores your workspace to the exact arrangement it was in when you exited the Desktop.

This arrangement (called *Startup* in the Layouts window) is not associated with a specific layout but is a feature of the Desktop operating environment. It can be thought of as a snapshot of your workspace at the last shutdown.

The contents of the icon bar are saved as part of a layout. Certain buttons or external commands in one layout may be useful only for certain tasks, and you may not need these in other layouts.

When you save a layout, you can only include windows controlled by the Desktop. You cannot save terminal emulator windows or other external program windows as part of your layout.

The layouts window shows available layouts in a list. Preconfigured layouts are in bold at the end of the list, and miniature icons at the left of their names contain a small padlock, indicating they cannot be removed or overwritten. The first item in the layouts list, Current, is highlighted. Current is not a layout; it identifies the arrangement of your workspace at this time, whether or not the arrangement is also a saved layout.

The second item, Startup, is also not a layout; it identifies the arrangement of your workspace when you started the current Desktop session, including arguments you specified if you started the Desktop from a command line.

Saving New Layouts. You can save many different layouts and switch between layouts as you perform different tasks in the Desktop. You can also specify one as the layout to use each time you start up the Desktop.

1. **In the Desktop window, organize your workspace the way you want it.**

   Open windows you want (including window attributes such as View, Positionable, Show Full Pathnames, or Sort key), place items on the Desktop you want to have accessible, and edit the icon bar if you want to show different buttons as part of a layout.

2. **Choose Layout | Layouts.**

The layouts window is displayed.

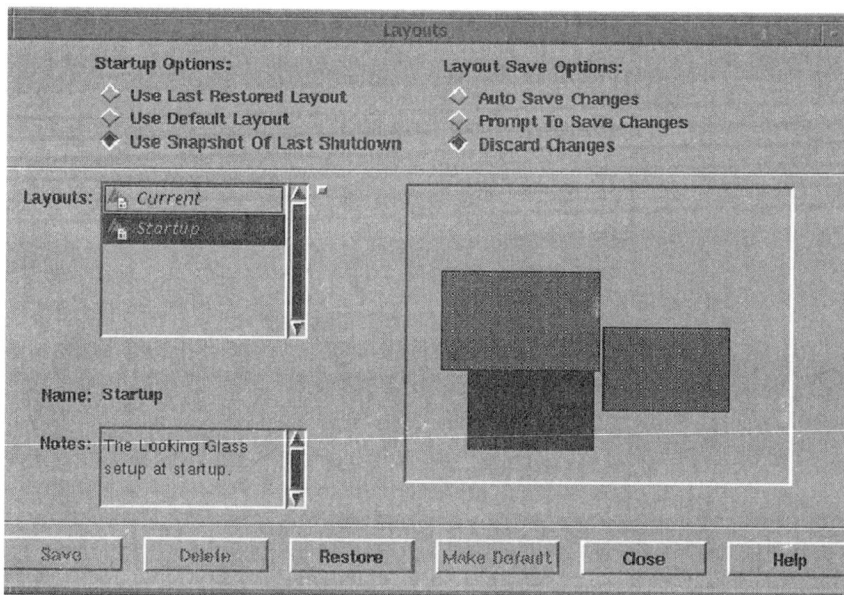

Figure 26: Layouts Window

3. **Click Current (the first item in the layouts list).**

The preview area at the right displays a thumbnail sketch of the workspace. The black rectangle represents the Desktop, the medium gray rectangles represent directory windows, and the light gray rectangles represent Desktop windows to be restored.

If you position the cursor over an item in the thumbnail sketch and press a mouse button, the name of that window appears beneath the preview area.

Some windows are not included precisely in Layout previews. The layering of windows when a layout is restored may not match the thumbnail sketch.

4. **Type the name of your new layout in the Name field.**

The layout name you specify can be up to 14 characters.

5. **(Optional) In the Notes field, type comments or notes you want for this layout.**

6. **Click Save to save your new layout.**

The new layout is saved and its name is added to the scrolling list. The name of the layout is also added to the Layout menu in the Desktop window.

You need to select the newly saved layout to restore it.

7. **Click Close to close the Layout window.**

Changing Saved Layouts. In the Layouts window, you can only save or change the current workspace arrangement as a layout. You must restore your workspace to that layout before making changes to it or saving it.

Specifying Layout Behavior. You can specify how the Desktop behaves at start-up and how it handles changes to your workspace as you move from layout to layout.

If you specify a default layout that the Desktop is to restore at start-up, it is identified by a check mark on its miniature icon at the left of its name in the Layouts window.

Using Environment Variables

This section discusses how to use the Environment Variables command from the Options menu in the Desktop window to work with environment variables.

What Are Environment Variables?

Environment variables provide a shorthand way to insert data into a command line or directory path and to pass information between programs.

Standard environment variables contain information about your operating environment. You cannot change or delete the names of some standard environment variables, but you can change their contents. In addition, you cannot change or delete the following (a lock appears beside their names in the list):

- HOME (the pathname of your home directory)
- PATH (your search path)
- TERM (your terminal type)

To use an environment variable in a text field or in another shell, enter a dollar sign ($) and the variable name. The Desktop, or another shell, substitutes the value of the variable at the point where the variable appears in the field.

The Desktop exports environment variables so that any program run by the Desktop inherits the current list of variables.

Editing Environment Variables

1. On the Desktop, select Options | Environment Variables.

    The Environment Variables window opens.

2.   From the list, select the variable you want to edit.

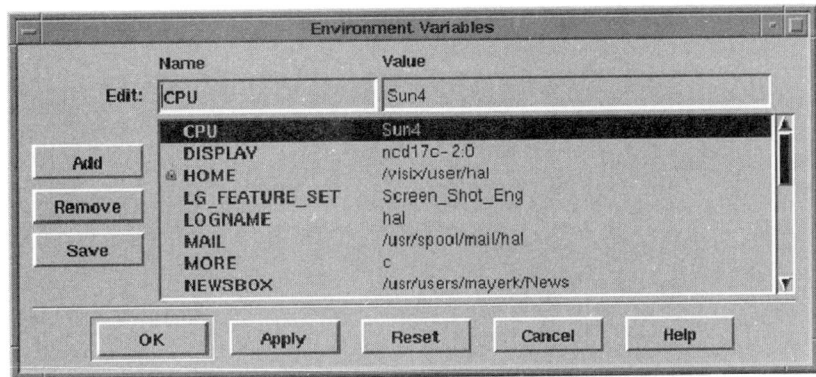

Figure 27: Environment Variables window

3.   (Optional) Edit the Name field.

4.   Edit the Value field to provide a value for the named variable.

5.   Choose Save to make your changes permanent.

6.   Choose one:

   • To apply changes and exit the Environment Variables window, click
     OK.

   • To apply changes without closing the window, click Apply.

   • To discard changes made since your environment variables were last
     saved, click Reset.

Adding Environment Variables

1.   On the Desktop, select Options | Environment Variables.

     The Environment Variables window opens.

2.   Click Add.

     A new variable called NEW_VAR_N is added to the list, and its value is
     listed as UNKNOWN.

3.   In the Name field, enter the name of the variable.

4.   In the Value field, enter the value for the variable.

5.   Choose one:

   •   To use the environment variable in a later Desktop session, click Save.

   •   To apply changes and exit the Environment Variables window, click OK.

   •   To apply changes without closing the window, click Apply.

Changing Desktop Preferences

The Desktop preferences let you specify how you want the Desktop to do certain things. There are several preference categories:

•   **Execution.** Use to specify which program to use to display terminal emulator windows, which text and data editors to use, which external shell to use, how to format and spool a file to be printed, and which pathname to use to receive mail.

•   **Operation.** Use to control the limit for file size, double-click speed, the action the Desktop performs when you double-click a directory, icon dragging behavior, which mouse behavior to use, and the seconds between display updates.

•   **Creation.** Use to define a creation mask that specifies default access permissions for new directories and files.

•   **Display.** Use to change the default characteristics of new directory windows, including their size, display format, and arrangement of directories and files.

•   **Removal.** Use to tell the Desktop when to ask for confirmation before removing individual or multiple directories or files, and whether or not to use the Desktop trash can when removing directories and files.

•   **Color.** Use to change the color of the Desktop interface elements.

•   **Sound.** Use to change the sounds associated with Desktop elements (if sound is available on your system).

- **Cleanup.** Use to change the grid on which directories and files are aligned when you use the Clean Up command in directory windows and on the Desktop.

All preferences are configured from the Preferences window, which you open by selecting Options | Preferences on the Desktop, or by using an icon on the icon bar.

You use the Desktop's Preferences window to access command windows in which you specify what to change. Double-click on any of the preferences in the preferences window to open a command window.

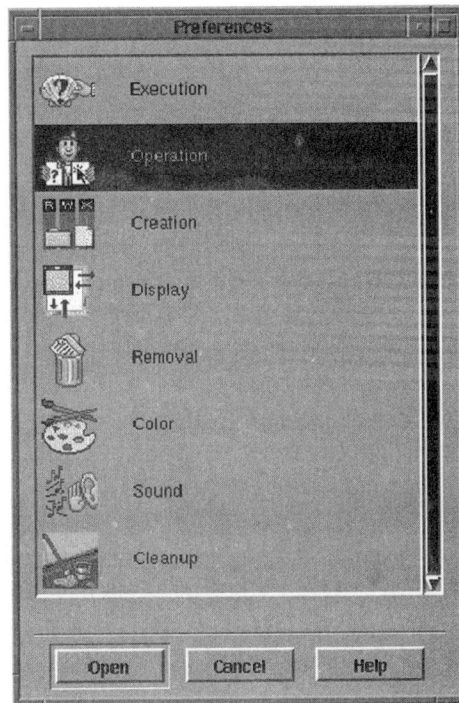

Figure 28: Preferences Scrolling List

Changing Execution Preferences

The Execution Preferences window specifies programs (and arguments) that the Desktop executes when you request certain operations. You can change the commands used for

- Emulating a terminal
- Editing a text file
- Editing a non-text (data) file
- Functions handled by an external shell
- Formatting and printing text files
- Receiving mail

When you select **Preferences | Execution**, the Execution Preferences window appears:

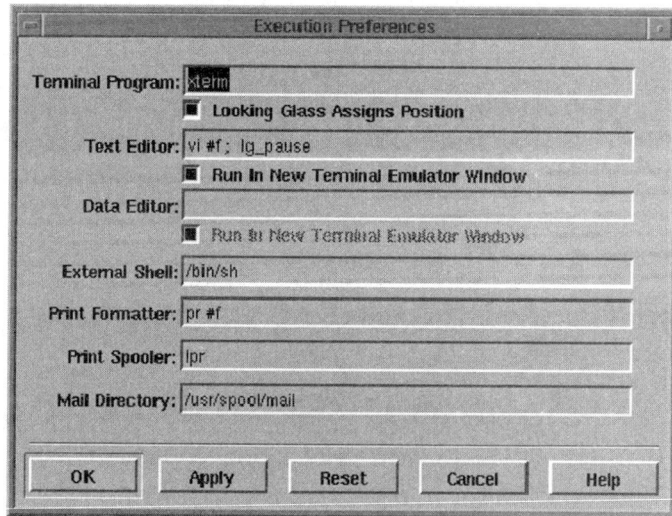

Figure 29: Execution Preferences

The Terminal Emulator. The Terminal Program field allows you to specify the pathname of the program you want the Desktop to execute when you select Run | Terminal Emulator, and when you use commands that must be run in a terminal emulator.

You can have the Desktop determine the position of terminal emulator windows on the workspace by selecting the Desktop Assigns Position checkbox (below the Terminal Program field). If the checkbox is not selected, the window manager determines the position.

You can specify a terminal program in Execution Preferences and include arguments you would use if you were invoking the program from a shell command prompt.

Specifying Text and Data Editors. The Execution Preferences Text Editor and Data Editor fields display the pathnames and arguments for the programs you want the Desktop to execute when you activate a text or data file.

To change a text or data editor, you must know the syntax used to invoke the program. If you enter just the pathname of the editor, the Desktop assumes it takes a file name as its only argument. For example, if in the Text Editor field you enter

```
/usr/bin/emacs #f
```

the Desktop executes the following command:

```
/usr/bin/emacs filename
```

when you activate (open or double-click) a text file (filename is the name of the file you selected).

To read exit messages from your editor or other program before its window disappears, put the lg_pause command after the command that calls the editor. The lg_pause command prompts you to press Enter before exiting the terminal emulator window.

When you use lg_pause, specify the position of the file name in the command line using the Desktop special symbol for selected files (#f). For example, to use the editor vi, select Run In New Terminal Emulator Window and enter the following in the Text Editor field:

```
/usr/bin/vi #f ; lg_pause
```

Note the use of the semicolon between the command that runs the editor and lg_pause. This causes lg_pause to run after the editor has exited.

Specifying an External Shell. The External Shell field displays the pathname of the shell the Desktop uses for any operation that requires an external shell, for many double-click actions, and for the Terminal Emulator command from the Desktop | Run menu.

You can change the shell if you prefer another. Otherwise, use the default shell, bash.

Specifying Commands for Printing. When the Desktop prints a file, it uses two commands: one to format the file and one to spool it to the printer. These two commands are displayed in the Print Formatter and Print Spooler fields in Execution Preferences.

The formatter command processes the file for printing—it might paginate the document or put in headers. The spooler command receives the data produced by the formatter command and sends it to the printer.

To determine the correct values for Print Formatter and Print Spooler, take the full command string you would normally use to print files and split it at the pipe symbol (|). Put the first half of the command in the Print Formatter field.

The Desktop assumes that the names of files to be printed are inserted at the end of the print command. If the names belong somewhere other than at the end, insert the special symbol for selected files (#f) where the file name should be placed. Put the second half of the command in the Print Spooler field.

The Desktop supplies the pipe symbol at execution time. For example, if you would print a file by entering on the command line

```
pr filename | lp
```

enter pr or pr #f in the Print Formatter field and lp in the Print Spooler field.

Changing Operation Preferences

The Operation Preferences window lets you control the following:

- The limit for file size
- The double-click speed
- The action the Desktop performs when you double-click a directory
- The appearance of icons during drag operations
- The mouse operation
- The seconds between display updates

When you select Preferences | Operation, the Operation Preferences window appears:

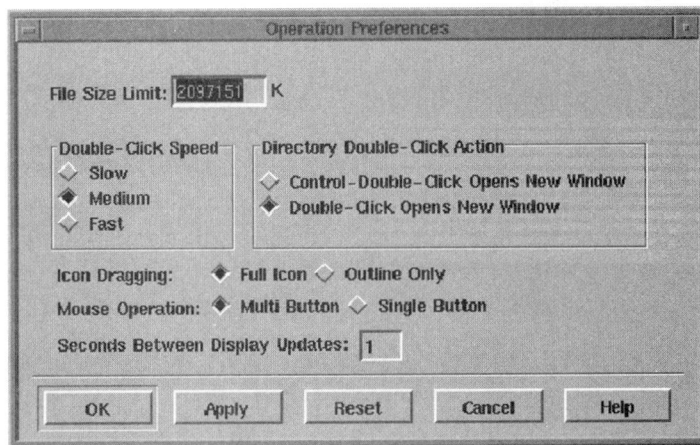

Figure 30: Operational Preferences

Specifying File Size Limit. To change the file size limit in the Desktop, choose Operation | File Size Limit. The size must be in 1K (1024 bytes) increments. Users can reduce the file size limit, but only the root user can increase the file size limit.

Specifying a Double-Click Speed. The Desktop lets you choose how fast or slow you can double-click a mouse button to get a double-click action instead of two single-click actions. The Desktop matches the time it takes you to double-click an object. The following options are available:

- **Slow** to allow a long amount of time between clicks
- **Medium** to allow a medium (or average) amount of time between clicks
- **Fast** to allow a very short amount of time between clicks

Specifying a Directory Double-Click Action. By default, the Desktop opens a directory window for each directory you double-click. However, if you Ctrl+double-click a directory, the Desktop displays the contents of that directory in the current directory window (no new window is opened).

In other words, the contents of the directory you double-click replace the contents of the directory displayed in that directory window.

Using Operation Preferences, you can indicate which double-click action you prefer as your default. You can specify whether to double-click or to Ctrl+double-click to open a new directory window.

Specifying an Icon Dragging Preference. For dragging operations, you can specify either of two behaviors: whether you want to display a full icon or only its outline during drag operations. Use the Icon Dragging radio buttons in Operation Preferences to specify

- **Full Icon**, for the Desktop to display the full icon image during drag operations.
- **Outline Only**, for the Desktop to display an outline of the icon during drag operations. Also, when you drag icons over drop receivers, only the cursor changes shape—the drop receiver icon does not change.

  On some systems, dragging an outline rather than the full icon can be a significant performance improvement, because the amount of redrawing done during a drag operation is greatly reduced.

Changing Creation Preferences

Use Creation Preferences to define a creation mask and default access permissions (protection modes) for new directories and files you create in the Desktop. A creation mask blocks permissions for new directories and files. Creation masks are important for maintaining security.

If you used the Desktop to set access permissions, you know that you select checkboxes to allow permissions. The creation mask works in the opposite way: you select checkboxes to exclude permissions.

For example, if you select the W (write) checkbox for Group when defining a creation mask, other members of your group will not be given write permission for files you create.

When you define a creation mask, you must tell the Desktop which creation mask to use when you start up the Desktop: the mask defined for that environment or a mask you want to define. To do this, you use the Store Mask or Inherit Mask buttons.

Default access permissions are automatically assigned to directories and files you create. Therefore, any permissions that you block using the creation mask will not become default access permissions.

When you select Preferences | Creation, the Creation Preferences window appears:

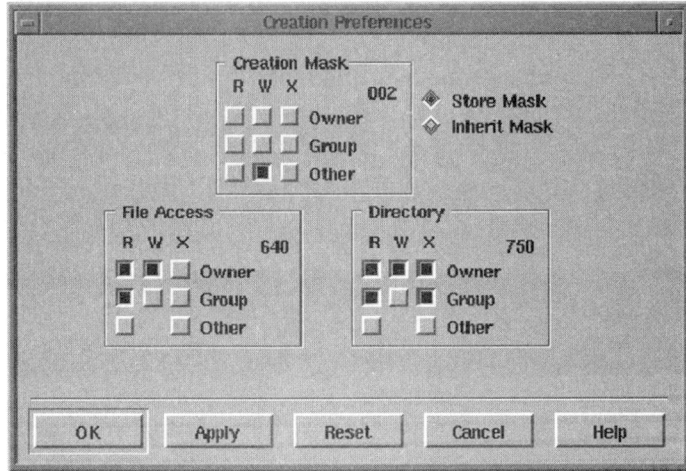

Figure 31: Creation Preferences

Changing Display Preferences

You can change the following default display options:

- How directory window titles are displayed
- The size of new directory windows
- Whether hidden files are displayed in directory windows
- The position of the splitter in new directory windows
- The display format for new directory windows
- How directories and files are arranged in directory windows when you use the Clean Up command

When you select Preferences | Display, the Display Preferences window appears:

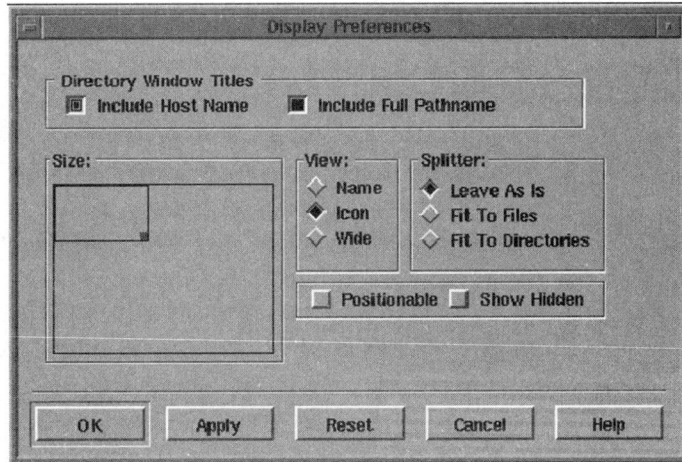

Figure 32: Display Preferences

Specifying How Directory Window Titles Are Displayed. In Display Preferences, in the Directory Window Titles section, you select

- **Include Host Name** to display in the title bar of each directory window the host name of the system you are logged into.
- **Include Full Pathname** to display in the title bar of each directory window the full pathname of the directory.

Specifying the Size of New Directory Windows. To specify proportionally the default size of new (or previously unopened) directory windows relative to your display, use the Display Preferences | Size. When a directory window opens, it will appear at the size you specify.

The rectangle on the left side of the window represents the size of a directory window. The larger, outer rectangle represents the size of your screen.

Specifying the Display Format for Directories and Files. Directories and files can be displayed in directory windows by name, icon, or in a wide format. Select one of the following:

- **Name** if you want directories and files displayed in alphabetical order by name
- **Icon** if you want to view directories and files by their icons
- **Wide** if you want to view directories and files in a wide, detailed format

Specifying Whether Directories and Files Are Positionable. When a directory window is in the non-positionable format, it contains a splitter. The splitter is a horizontal bar that divides the window into two sections. The top section contains subdirectories; the bottom section contains files.

Use Display Preferences to change the default so that directory windows open without the splitter and so directories and files are displayed together. They can then be positioned anywhere in their windows.

Specifying Whether Hidden Files Are Displayed in Directory Windows.

Hidden files are directories and files whose names begin with "." (with the exception of the current and parent directories). These directories and files are not shown by default because the "." prefix is often used in naming system configuration files or data files that users rarely need to view.

You can use Display Preferences to change the default so that hidden files are displayed when a directory window opens.

Changing Removal Preferences

The Removal Preferences settings tell the Desktop how to handle trash removal and when to ask you for confirmation before removing directories and files. There are three groups of removal options, one for each of the following:

- Trash

- Files
- Directories.

When you select Preferences | Removal, the Removal Preferences window appears:

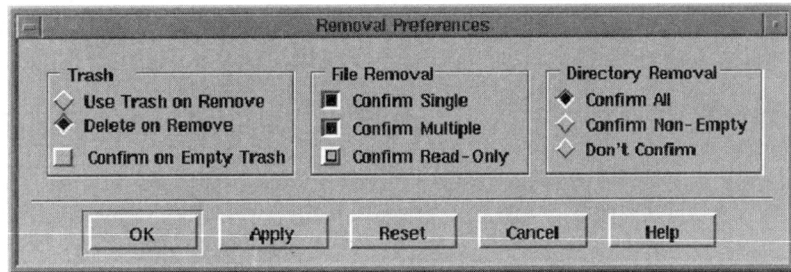

Figure 33: Removal Preferences

Setting Removal Preferences. When you remove a selected object using File | Remove, the object can be permanently removed or it can be placed in the trash can. Items in the trash can be recovered until the can is emptied, which is safer when removing files. You choose between:

- **Use Trash On Remove** if you want each file or directory removed to be put into the trash can. (You can retrieve items in the trash before the trash is emptied.)
- **Delete On Remove** if you want the Desktop to delete each file or directory when you remove it, bypassing the trash can.

In the File Removal group, check any of the following:

- **Confirm Single** for the Desktop to ask you for confirmation before it removes each file
- **Confirm Multiple** for the Desktop to ask you for confirmation before it removes more than one file in a single operation
- **Confirm Read-Only** for the Desktop to ask you for confirmation before it removes files with read-only protection

In the Directory Removal group, select one of the following:

- **Confirm All** for the Desktop to ask you for confirmation before it removes each directory

- **Confirm Non-Empty** for the Desktop to ask you for confirmation before it removes each directory that contains subdirectories or files

- **Don't Confirm** to never have the Desktop ask you for confirmation before it removes a directory

Changing Color Preferences

If you have a color monitor, you can change the colors of interface elements by using Preferences | Color. (If you do not have a color monitor, color preferences are disabled.) You can change the color of the following elements:

- **Background**, the *canvas* that objects are drawn on; for example, the workspace area behind directories and files displayed on the Desktop.

- **Foreground**, what is drawn on the canvas; for example, text, icons, buttons, and checkboxes.

- **Top shadow**, the shadow that appears on the top and left edges of three-dimensional objects.

- **Bottom shadow,** the shadow that appears on the bottom and right edges of three-dimensional objects.

The following example identifies background, foreground, top shadow, and bottom shadow elements:

Figure 34: Example of background, foreground, top shadow, and bottom shadow elements.

The following paragraphs give you guidelines for setting color preferences.

If you use a two-dimensional appearance, make sure the foreground color stands out well against the background color. If you use the three-dimensional appearance, make the top shadow the lightest color of the four, and use a color similar to the background.

For example, if you set the background to blue, the top shadow should be a much lighter blue; the bottom shadow should be the darkest color, similar to the background, but much darker. The foreground color should stand out well against the background color.

You can specify colors by adjusting values in any of four models:

- The hue, light, and saturation (HLS) model
- The red, green, blue (RGB) model
- The cyan, magenta, yellow (CMY) model
- The greyscale model

Accessing the Color Preferences Window. Set color preferences by choosing Preferences | Color. When you open Color Preferences, the colors in use by the four Desktop user interface elements are shown:

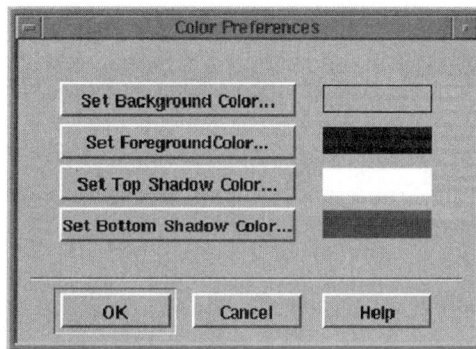

Figure 35: Color Preferences Window

To adjust the color, select one of these buttons and then set the color by choosing a model to set the color by clicking its button at the top of the

Select Color window, shown below. (RGB, CMY, and greyscale are available, in addition to HLS shown in the figure.)

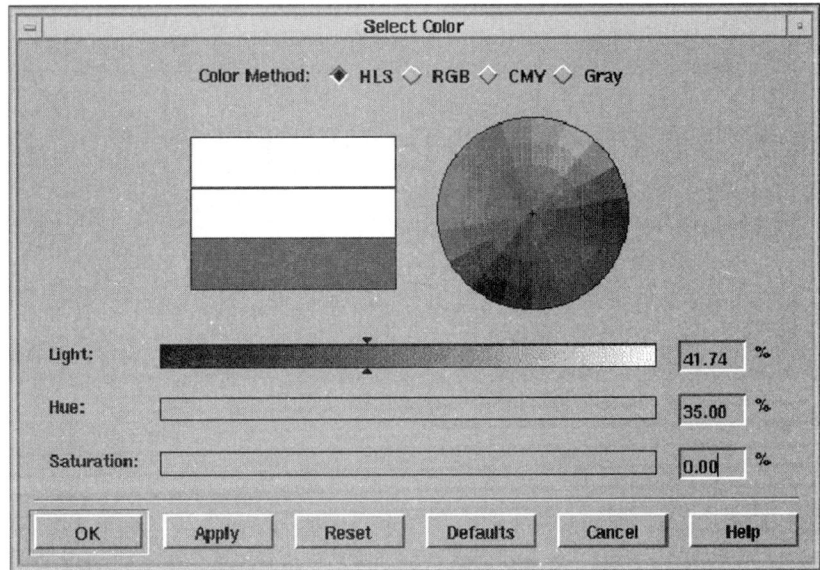

Figure 36: HLS screen

Changing a Desktop Color

1. In Color Preferences, choose a system color to set (for example, the foreground color).

    The Select Color window opens.

2. At the top of the window, choose the color model that you prefer to work in (HLS, RGB, CMY, or Greyscale)

3. Select the appropriate values by dragging the sliders, clicking in the color wheel, or entering values in the fields.

    The New section displays the color you create.

4. To save changes and exit Color Preferences, click OK; to save changes without closing the window, click Apply; to revert to the system standard color preferences, click Defaults.

Changing Cleanup Preferences

Cleanup preferences let you control the grid that directories and icons line up on when you use the Clean Up command in a directory window.

When you select Preferences | Cleanup, the Cleanup Preferences window appears:

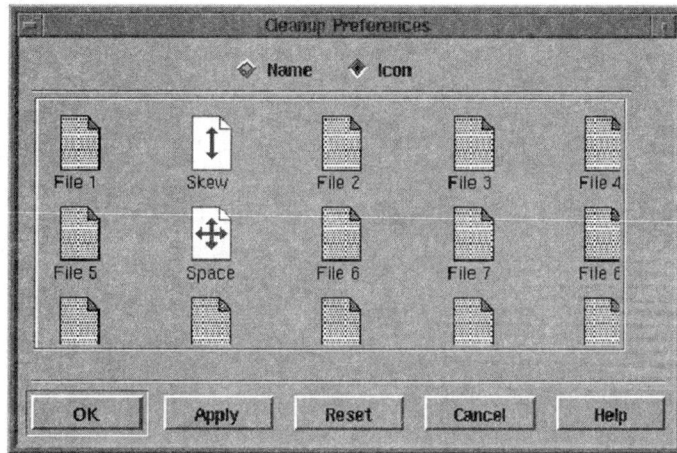

Figure 37: Cleanup Preferences

Setting Cleanup Preferences

1. Select one of the following:

   - **Name** to change how directories and files are displayed in Name view when cleaned up

   - **Icon** to change how directories and files are displayed in Icon view when cleaned up

   The preview area contains small icons for Name view and large icons for Icon view. The top two icons in the second column are named Skew and Space. When you click one of these objects, your cursor turns into an arrow that shows which direction you can move the object.

2. Drag one of the following:

- **Skew** to move the column of objects up or down so that every other column is staggered
- **Space** to move objects closer or farther apart

3. **To save changes and exit Cleanup Preferences, click OK; to save changes without closing the window, click Apply; to change the grid in the preview area to its original layout without closing the window, click Reset.**

File Typing on the Desktop

This section describes how file typing works and the general capabilities of the file typing language. File typing is done automatically when you use the Desktop. Adding to the file typing capabilities is a task for advanced users; only an overview of the features of file typing is included here. More detailed information on file typing, and a complete reference of available file typing commands and examples are available in the online *Desktop User Guide*.

How File Typing Works

The Desktop's file typing mechanism consists of three basic components:

- A file typing language (FTL), used to define the rules by which file types are identified
- A file typing compiler (FTC), which compiles file typing rules written using the FTL
- A file system server (FSS), which manages file system information and allows high-speed access to directories

File type definitions are written in text files using the FTL. They include statements that describe files (such as a particular format for a file name), a string of characters that must be in a specific location in the file, or a location in the file system in which the directory or file must be found.

In addition to the rules used to determine file types, file type definitions specify the icon to display for each directory or file and actions associated with that type of file.

These definitions are compiled by the FTC to create a binary file named LG_rulebase. LG_rulebase is stored in the Desktop data directory (specified at installation) and is read into memory at start-up.

When the Desktop displays the contents of a directory, the FSS looks for an .lgdb file. If this file is not found, the file type information for every file in the directory is computed. If the user has write permission for the directory, an .lgdb file is created for use the next time the Desktop opens the directory.

If an .lgdb file is present, the FSS compares the contents of the .lgdb file to the contents of the directory to determine whether directories or files were added to the directory since the last time the .lgdb file was modified.

If so, newly added items are typed according to the current rulebase. If the current user has write permission for the .lgdb file (the normal situation), it is updated.

Adding New File Typing Rules

Though a complete description of available commands and features is not provided in this chapter, you can still try adding simple file types by imitating existing file types. Use the procedure below, referring to the more in-depth online instructions as needed.

1. **Review the system rulebase files for something similar to what you want to add to the rulebase.**

    Rulebase files are stored in the directory /usr/visix/lg/default/lg_ftc. Rules for programs are in prog.ftc; rules for other files are in data.ftc. You should store your new rules in the corresponding files, prog.loc.ftc and data.loc.ftc.

2. Copy a rule that is similar to what you need from the appropriate rulebase file (prog.ftc or data.ftc) to the appropriate rulebase file (prog.loc.ftc or data.loc.ftc).

3. Modify the new rule to fit your needs.

4. Save and exit the rulebase file.

5. Compile and install the new rulebase files by entering these two commands while you are still in the lg_ftc directory:

```
make
```

```
make install
```

6. Exit the Desktop and restart it to have your new rules take effect.

CHAPTER 6

Working With Internet and Intranet Services

Caldera OpenLinux is ideal for providing Information services to your organization as an Intranet or Internet server. Though complete information about setting up and managing these information services is beyond the scope of this chapter, the following sections explain briefly how Open-Linux can be configured and used:

- IP Configuration
- Basic Routing and Name Services
- Providing Services to an Intranet
- Providing Services on the Internet
- Network Information Services
- Client Access to Network Information Services

Becoming a full-fledged Internet server with things like a Web server, email access for clients, and an FTP site is not a trivial task. After you read through this chapter to learn the basics, you can find more assistance by looking in following sources.

- The online documentation included on the Caldera CD-ROM. In particular, consult the Linux Documentation Project HOWTO documents, and the man pages for the services described (for example, enter the command man ftpd).
- A Caldera Channel Partner, who may specialize in setup or administration of Internet and Intranet services.
- Additional reference materials from the Internet, your Internet Service Provider, or your local computer bookstore.

IP Network Configuration

The Internet Protocol (IP) is the basis for all networking done on the Internet. The IP information needed to configure your system was requested during the installation process. That configuration information is sufficient if you want to be a client on the Internet. If you want to use OpenLinux to operate an Internet server, you need to complete addition configuration, as described in the sections below.

If you need to alter the IP networking information that you entered during installation, this section describes how to use the graphical networking configuration tools to do so.

The network configuration utility is shown below. If you logged in as root, an icon for this utility is shown on your Desktop. You must be logged in as root to change IP networking. The IP networking parameters that you can edit are described in the paragraphs below.

You can also use the LISA utility to configure your IP networking.

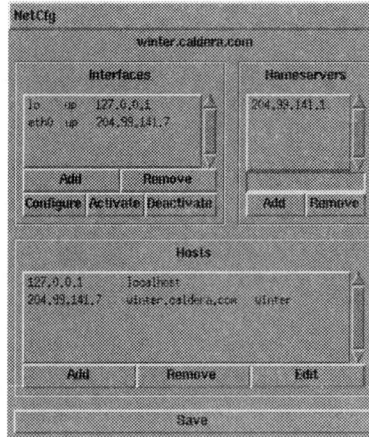

- Interfaces

  Network devices can be added, removed, configured, brought up, brought down, etc. Ethernet, loopback, PPP and SLIP devices are supported.

  If you are using SLIP configuration, you should edit */etc/dip-script* to "chat" properly with your SLIP server. Carefully check the wait lines, which must recognize what your SLIP server says.

- Nameservers

  You can add nameservers to this dialog. These will be used to resolve domain names.

- Hosts

  You can add specific computers to the list of Hosts. The names in this list include an IP address, and are used to resolve the listed domain names when a name server is not available.

- Hostname

  You can change the name of your system. Changing your hostname could cause problems if other systems are using your system by referring to its name (for example, as a Worldwide Web or FTP server).

Editing Network Parameters

1. Start the graphical Network Configuration utility by choosing it on the Desktop.

   If you do not have an icon for the Network Configuration utility on your Desktop, you can enter the following command within a graphical terminal emulator window (such as xterm):

   ```
   netcfg
   ```

2. Select the parameter that you wish to edit, as described in the list of parameters above.

   a. If you wish to add a parameter, an Add dialog will open when you choose the corresponding Add button.

   b. If you wish to delete a parameter, select that parameter in the list before choosing the Remove button.

   c. If you wish to edit the hostname, choose Edit Hostname from the menu.

3. Choose the Save button to make your changes permanent.

4. Choose the Done button to exit the utility.

Basic Routing and Name Services

In order to communicate with other computers by using their IP addresses, one computer must have a method of discovering the IP address of another computer. This is done through IP routing. Routing involves one computer keeping track of how to locate other computers, and passing that information on when requested to do so.

Routing

Routing can apply to many protocols. This section refers to routing IP packets, which are what the Internet and the information services described in this chapter use.

The computer that routed packets on a network was traditionally separate from the computers on which people did their daily work. The router sat in a closet and did nothing but receive IP packets and send them on according to various routing protocols. On a busy network, it is still helpful to have a dedicated router to manage the large number of packets to be routed.

On smaller networks, particularly those not connected to the Internet (perhaps providing Internet-type information services internally), a dedicated router is not needed. The routing functionality of OpenLinux can fill this need without dedicating a separate computer as a router.

As installed by default, OpenLinux performs many routing functions. To act as a gateway from computers in your organization to the Internet, or from outside computers that dial-up to your server (via PPP), you must also have IP forwarding. IP forwarding is a routing feature that is included in OpenLinux, but is not turned on after initially installing it.

To activate IP forwarding, you must go to the directory /usr/src/linux and enter the command make config. The process that this command starts is quite complicated. If you are unfamiliar with routing or using UNIX tools, we recommend contacting your ISP or a Caldera Channel Partner for information.

Name Services

In addition to the IP address of a computer, we often refer to a computer by its hostname and domain name. These names, while useful for us, are not understood by other computers. They must be converted into IP addresses. The programs that do this conversion are providing *Name Services*.

In the same way that a router provides information on IP addresses to other computers, a name server provides conversions for other computers that have a host or domain name and want an IP address. The name server keeps tables of how to convert many names, and where to send requests that it does not have a conversion for.

The simplest form of name service is the file /etc/hosts on your Caldera system. This file can list host and domain names with their IP addresses. This file usually contains few entries, however, because you usually don't know the IP numbers of all the computers on the Internet that you want to contact.

OpenLinux includes complete functionality for the Domain Name Services (DNS) and Network Information Services (NIS). Setting up these services is beyond the scope of this book. Learning more about the following commands can help you get started, however. Use the man command with each one to learn more (for example, enter the command man named). In addition, review the files in the directory /etc/named/boot.

- ifconfig
- route
- named
- bind
- dig
- nslookup
- whois

Providing Services to an Intranet

If you have set up networking (routing with IP forwarding and DNS name server), all network information services are be available to anyone on your network that uses IP networking.

To provide information services, review the various sections in this chapter to learn about setting up the services you want to have available on your system, then tell people in your organization about them and how to use them.

For example, The Web server is set up by default, you can start giving everyone the name of the computer on which the Web server is running, and they can start retrieving documents.

Providing Services on the Internet

Providing information services to the Internet is really no different from providing them to your local organization. The only additional concerns are the security of information on your network, and expanding your networking connectivity to include the Internet.

Getting Connected

Vendors of a variety of Internet-related hardware have begun to provide Linux drivers for their equipment. These drivers enable OpenLinux to provide the most cost-effective high-speed connections to the Internet. Support for Frame Relay cards, ISDN cards, multi-port serial cards, and related systems allow systems integrators to provide a complete Internet solution on Caldera OpenLinux without costly external hardware components or software add-ons. Information about these hardware products is included on the Caldera Web page.

Dedicated Internet Connections

If you wish to create an Internet site that you anticipate will have high traffic, you should connect to the Internet via a high-speed, dedicated communications line. OpenLinux can easily be connected to this type of line with an expansion board (no additional software is needed). For information on creating such a connection to the Internet, contact a Caldera Channel Partner or your Internet Service Provider.

SLIP and PPP

You can also connect directly to the Internet via your modem using the Serial Line Internet Protocol (SLIP) or the Point to Point Protocol (PPP). The software to use SLIP and PPP are included with OpenLinux. You will need an account with an Internet Service Provider that uses SLIP or PPP, however.

Information about setting up SLIP and PPP is provided in the Linux Documentation Project (LDP) HOWTO sections. These documents are included on the CD-ROM.

Allowing Access to Services

As a security measure, most network services are managed by a protective program called a TCP wrapper. The protected services are those listed in the *etc/inetd.conf* file which use the */usr/sbin/tcpd* program. These services include, for example, FTP and Worldwide Web (HTTP) access.

The tcpd program can allow or deny access to a service based on the origin of the request. This is a security feature to prevent you from installing OpenLinux and suddenly having the world begin to read your files. To enable services, you can edit the */etc/hosts.allow* file. This file, when edited to allow access to services, might look like this:

```
ALL: mycompany.com .mycompany.com

in.talkd: ALL

in.ntalkd: ALL

in.fingerd: ALL

in.ftpd: ALL .
```

This configuration allows all connections from mycompany.com and *.mycompany.com machines. It also allows the services talk, finger, and ftp to accept requests from all machines.

The tcpd program allows much more sophisticated access control, using a combination of the files */etc/hosts.allow* and */etc/hosts.deny.* Read the tcpd(8) and hosts_access(5) man pages for complete details.

Modem Pools

OpenLinux is ideal for those who wish to provide modem pools for users to connect to a network via a standard telephone line. Each modem uses a serial port. Cards with multiple serial ports are available from several manufacturers, and can provide from 4 to 256 serial ports through a single expansion slot on your PC.

Network Information Services

The reason people want to connect to the Internet is because of the services that it provides. In this section, we describe the most popular services that you may want to provide on your Internet server. OpenLinux includes full capabilities in all of the services described below (and in many less popular services as well).

- Email

  Email is used to send messages from one person to one or a few others, directly from machine to machine. It is not a real-time transfer, but offers the advantage of being able to pass through several intermediate machines to reach the addressee. Email on OpenLinux and the Internet uses the protocol SMTP.

- FTP

  The File Transfer Protocol is used to transfer files from a centralized repository to a client located on the network. In practice, FTP servers (repositories) exist all over the world, each providing files that their owners want to make available. FTP is designed for direct, real-time access, but without interacting with the information being transferred. The protocol used is actually called FTP.

- Worldwide Web

The Web uses the protocol HTTP to access small to medium sized documents with a direct, real-time connection to another computer on the network. It is similar to the uses of FTP, but HTTP is designed to allow the person receiving the file to immediately interact with the file received. In conjunction with HTTP and the Web, a format for the documents transferred is defined: HTML. This format is suited to interactive, graphical documents.

- NFS

  The Network File System protocol is used to access part of a remote filesystem as if it were part of your local filesystem. NFS is not commonly used across the Internet because of security and speed issues, but it can be when needed.

- News

  The Usenet newsgroups are like a giant communal email system, divided by subjects. Users can read messages submitted by others, and submit their own messages, which everyone can read. Using the protocol NNTP, the newsgroup messages are copied from server to server (mirrored) so that users can quickly access them.

Email

OpenLinux works very well as an organizational mail server and gateway. The following summary information describes using OpenLinux as an email gateway using the sendmail program. If you require further reference on email or sendmail, we recommend the book *sendmail*, by Bryan Costales, from O'Reilly & Associates, Inc., and the documentation for sendmail, written by the author of sendmail.

sendmail Configuration

A default sendmail.cf configuration file is placed in */etc* during installation. The default configuration should work for most SMTP-only sites. It will not work for UUCP sites; you must generate a new sendmail.cf if you need to use UUCP mail transfers.

To generate a sendmail.cf, install the following packages from the Caldera CD-ROM:

- m4
- sendmail sources

Read the README in */usr/src/mail/sendmail-8.6.9/cf* for more details on creating sendmail configuration files.

One common sendmail configuration is to have a single machine act as a mail gateway for all the machines on your network. For instance, the main organizational Internet gateway, company.com, often handles all mail accounts. We can add the hostnames of other machines in the organization to the */etc/sendmail.cw* files, in order to have mail sent to those machines captured by the main mail server company.com. For example, we might add the following lines to sendmail.cw:

```
# sendmail.cw - include all aliases for your
machine.

torgo.company.com

poodle.company.com

devel.company.com
```

Then on the other machines (torgo, poodle, and devel), we would edit the */etc/sendmail.cf* file to "masquerade" as company.com when sending mail, and to forward any local mail processing to company.com. To do this, find the DH and DM lines in */etc/sendmail.cf* and edit them:

```
# who gets all local email traffic ($R has prece-
dence for unqualified names)

 DHcompany.com

 # who I masquerade as (null for no masquerading)

DMcompany.com
```

With this type of configuration, all mail sent will appear as if it were sent from company.com and any mail sent to torgo.company.com or the other hosts, will be delivered to company.com.

Setting Up an FTP Server

An FTP server is automatically set up as part of the standard OpenLinux installation. This server can be used for anonymous FTP as well. For information about configuring your FTP server, use the command man ftpd.

Setting Up a Worldwide Web Server

A Worldwide Web server is automatically started on OpenLinux to provide online help and documentation. If you wish to use this Web server to provide documents to others, all you need to do is place the documents in the correct directory. The default directory for these document files is /home/httpd/html. You must be connected to the Internet for users to access your computer.

Your OpenLinux Lite CD-ROM includes the Apache Web server software, which can be used for multiple domain names. For example, your could advertise both *CompanyA.com* and *CompanyB.com* as Web addresses, while hosting both sites on the same OpenLinux computer.

The configuration files for the Web server are already set up so that all users can see your Web server. They can only see the files in the document directory of the Web server, however. You can change the configuration files for the Web server as needed. They are located in /etc/httpd/conf.

To provide information to other users via the Worldwide Web, just check the following points:

- Place Web documents (in HTML format) in the default Web document directory, */home/httpd/html.*
- Have a network connection to the users who want to access your Web server (this is usually an Internet connection).

Setting Up NFS Services

All the required NFS daemons are started at boot time by default. The portmapper which controls access to NFS services, however, utilizes the /

etc/hosts.allow and */etc/hosts.deny* files for access control. To enable other machines to mount a directory from your system via NFS, you must add a line to */etc/hosts.allow* for each machine or domain which you wish to allow to connect to the portmapper.

In order to avoid deadlocks, the portmap program does not attempt to look up the remote host name or user name, nor will it try to match NIS netgroups. Thus only network number patterns (IP addresses) will work for portmap access control. For example, to allow all hosts in the madison.com domain (whose network address is 194.143.24.0), you would add the following line to */etc/hosts.allow*:

```
portmap: 194.143.24.0/255.255.255.0
```

See the hosts_access(5) and rpc.portmap(8) man pages for complete access control details.

To export a filesystem via NFS, so that other systems can mount it, include the directory where the filesystem is mounted on your system in the */etc/exports.* directory. For example, to allow hosts matching *.madison.com to mount */mnt/rhscd* and */mnt/cdrom* as read-only filesystems, first add these lines to the */etc/exports* file:

```
/mnt/rhscd          *.madison.com(ro)

/mnt/cdrom          *.madison.com(ro)
```

Then kill and restart the rpc.nfsd and rpc.mountd daemons so that they will load the new configuration. See the exports(5), rpc.nfsd(8) and rpc.mountd(8) man pages for complete details.

Setting Up a News Server

OpenLinux is well-suited to act as a newsgroup server for your organization. The CD-ROM includes all of the software components to set up OpenLinux as an NNTP-based news server, allowing users to read news and post to the thousands of Internet newsgroups.

All that you need is an Internet connection, and the expertise to set up the news server. Setting up a news server is a complex operation, and is beyond the scope of this book. We recommend that you contact your network administrator, or consult the reference books mentioned at the beginning of this chapter.

Client Access to Network Information Services

If your network has an Internet connection, you can immediately begin accessing Internet resources when you have installed OpenLinux. Simply execute one of the Internet services commands such as telnet or ftp, or double-click on the browser icon located on the Desktop.

The Web browser included with OpenLinux Lite provides graphical client access to many services, including:

- Worldwide Web
- FTP
- gopher

If you prefer not to work in a graphical environment, you can also access Internet information systems with the following character-based utilities by entering the command name in a terminal window:

- elm is used to read and send email
- trn is used to read newsgroups
- ftp is used to access ftp sites

Hardware Parameters

The auto-detect feature of the Installation program should determine exactly what hardware you have and allow the installation of Caldera OpenLinux to proceed without problems.

Occasionally, however, the auto-detection feature needs some "help" to correctly locate and use your hardware. If necessary, you provide this help by entering boot parameters when you start the installation process, or kernel parameters (called insmod parameters) when using the Kernel Module Manager during installation.

Each parameter indicates a type of hardware (or other option) and one or more values that identify that hardware or option so that it can be correctly used. Boot parameters are entered at the boot manager prompt, before the OpenLinux installation actually starts. The insmod parameters are entered during installation, when prompted from the Kernel Module Manager menus.

For example, at the LILO boot manager prompt, you might normally enter linux (or press Enter if linux is the default).

    LILO: linux

If you determine during installation that boot parameters are needed, you might enter something like this instead:

    LILO: linux cdu31a=0x340,13 eth0=11,0x260,0,0,eth0

This example indicates the addressing information for a Sony CD-ROM drive and an ethernet card. The equal sign (=) separates the parameter from the value you provide. Spaces separate multiple parameters.

You can also use boot parameters to turn off the auto-detection feature if needed. For example, if the auto-detection feature checks for some types of CD-ROM drives, it may interfere with the configuration of some network cards as a side effect. You can overcome this by providing information about your CD-ROM drive and turning off the auto-detection, thus maintaining your network card configuration.

Below are some recommended boot and insmod parameters to help you access and configure hardware that may not respond well to the auto-detection. To use parameters, you may need to know information such as the IRQ interrupt and memory address used by your hardware. Consult your hardware documentation or call your manufacturer. If you have DOS already configured on your computer, you may be able to discover some relevant hardware information by reviewing the CONFIG.SYS file in DOS.

Items enclosed in square brackets in the syntax diagrams are optional when you enter your parameters. Items in the syntax descriptions that are in italics are variables for which you must supply a value.

A device generally has only one boot parameter, which may have several value pairs. A kernel module can have several different parameters that all apply to the same device.

After entering one of these parameters at the boot manager prompt, watch the kernel messages to see if the device was recognized correctly. Messages will generally either have "failed" or a display of the device with the correct port, IRQ, etc.

After the device-specific listings are several additional setting that you can use to control the action of the kernel and device modules during start-up.

CD-ROM Parameters

ISP16/MAD16/Mozart soft configurable CD-ROM

- type: cdrom (1)
- kernel module: isp16
- boot parameters: isp16=IO[,IRQ[,DMA]]][,TYPE]
- possible insmod parameters:
  isp16_cdrom_base={[0x340],0x320,0x330,0x360}
  isp16_cdrom_irq={[0],3,5,7,9,10,11}
  isp16_cdrom_dma={[0],3,5,6,7}
  isp16_cdrom_type={noisp16,[Sanyo],Panasonic,Sony,Mitsumi}
  (noisp16 disables driver)

Sony CDU31A/CDU33A

- type: cdrom (2)
- kernel module: cdu31a
- boot parameters: cdu31a=iobase,[irq[,is_pas_card]]
  iobase={0x320,0x330,0x340,0x360,0x634,0x654,0x1f88}
  irq={-1,[0],3,4,5,6}
  -1 is to scan
  0 is for no irq
  is_pas_card={0,1} for Pro Audio Spectrum Card
- possible insmod parameters:
  cdu31a_port={0x320,0x330,0x340,0x360,0x634,0x654,0x1f88}
  cdu31a_irq={-1,[0],3,4,5,6}

sony_pas_init={0,1}

Mitsumi FX001S/D (non IDE/ATAPI)

- type: cdrom (3)
- kernel module: mcd
- boot parameters: mcd=IO,IRQ,FLAG
    IO={[0x300],..,0x3FC} (in 0x04 steps)
    IRQ={3,5,9,[10],11}
    FLAG={[0],1}
- possible insmod parameters:
    mcd_port={[0x300],..,0x3FC} (in 0x04 steps)
    mcd_irq={3,5,9,[10],11}
    mitsumi_bug_93_wait=

Mitsumi XA/MultiSession (non IDE/ATAPI)

- type: cdrom (4)
- kernel module: mcdx
- boot parameter: mcdx=IO
- possible insmod parameters:
    mcdx=IO

Matsushita/Panasonic/Teac/CreativeLabs on SBPRO (non IDE/ATAPI)

- type: cdrom (5)
- kernel module: sbpcd
- boot parameters: sbpcd=IO,TYPE
    IO={0x...}   default: 0x340
    TYPE={LaserMate,SoundBlaster,SoundScape,Teac16bit}
- possible insmod parameters:
    IO={0x...}
    TYPE={0,1,2,3}

For TYPE, 0=LaserMate, 1=SoundBlaster, 2=SoundScape, 3= Teac16bit

Aztech/Orchid/Okano/Wearnes/Conrad/TXC/CyDROM (non IDE)

- type: cdrom (6)
- kernel module: aztcd
- boot parameters: aztcd=iobase[,magic_number]
  iobase={[0x320"],?}
  magic_number=0x79
- possible insmod parameters:
  aztcd=iobase[,magic_number]

Sony CDU535

- type: cdrom (7)
- kernel module: sonycd535
- boot parameters: "sonycd535=IO[,IRQ]
  IO={noprobe,0x340,?}
  noprobenoprobe disables driver
  IRQ={...}
- possible insmod parameters:
  sonycd535=ADR
  (sonycd535_cd_base_io={0x340,?}
  (sonycd535_irq_used={...}?)

GoldStar R420

- type: cdrom (8)
- kernel module: gscd
- boot parameters: gscd=IO
- possible insmod parameters:
  gscd={0x300,0x310,0x320,0x330,[0x340],0x350,0x360,0x370,0x380,
  0x390, 0x3A0,0x3B0,0x3C0,0x3D0,0x3E0,0x3F0}

Philips/LMS CM206/226 on CM260

- type: cdrom (9)
- kernel module: cm206
- boot parameters: cm206=IO,IRQ
  IO={0x300,..,[0x340],..,0x370}
  IRQ={3..[11]}
  auto
- possible insmod parameters:
  cm206=IO,IRQ
  cm206=auto

Optics Storage DOLPHIN 8000AT

- type: cdrom (10)
- kernel module: optcd
- boot parameter: optcd=IO
  IO={0x340,?}
- possible insmod parameters:
  optcd=IO

Sanyo CDR-H94A

- type: cdrom (11)
- kernel module: sjcd
- boot parameters: sjcd=IO[,IRQ[,DMAl]]
  IO={[0x340],?}
  IRQ={[0]}
  DMA={[0]}
- possible insmod parameters:
  sjcd_base=IO

SCSI Parameters

AdvanSys ABPxxx

- type: scsi (1)
- kernel module: advansys
- boot parameters: advansys=IO,IO2,IO3,IO4,DEBUGLEVEL

  IO=0x...   IO Port of 1st adapter

  IO2=0x...   IO Port of 2nd adapter

  IO3=0x...   IO Port of 3rd adapter

  IO4=0x...   IO Port of 4th adapter

  DEBUGLEVEL=0xdeb{0..F)
- possible insmod parameters:

  asc_ioport=IO[,IO2,IO3,IO4]

  asc_dbglevel=DEBUGLEVEL

  asc_iopflag=(0,1)   disables or enables port scanning

  asc_ioport={[0x110],0x130,0x150,0x190,0x210,0230,0x250,0x330}

  asc_dbglevel={0..N}

      0=Errors only, 1=High-level tracing, 2+=Verbose tracing

BusLogic

- type: scsi (2)
- kernel module: BusLogic
- boot parameters: BusLogic=IO, TAGGED_QUEUE, BUS_SETTLE, LOCAL_OPT, GLOBAL_OPT, STRINGS
- possible insmod parameters:

  IO_Address={0x330,0x334,0x230,0x234,0x130,0x134}

  TaggedQueueDepth=

  BusSettleTime=

  LocalOptions=

  BusLogic_GlobalOptions=|= assignment

  TQ:[Default,Enable,Disable]set TaggedQueuingPermitted

ER:[Default,HardReset,BusDeviceReset,None]

NoProbe

noprobe

NoProbeISA

NoSortPCI

Ultrastor 14f (ISA), 24f (EISA), 34f (VLB)

- type: scsi (3)
- kernel module: u14-34f
- boot parameters: *none*
- insmod parameters: *none*

UltraStore

- type: scsi (4)
- kernel module: ultrastor
- boot parameters:
- possible insmod parameters:
  io_ports={[0x330],0x340,0x310,0x230,0x240,0x210,0x130,0x140}
  dma_list={5,6,7,0}
  irq_list={10,11,14,[15]}

Adaptec AHA152X

- type: scsi (5)
- kernel module: aha152x
- boot parameters: aha152x=IO, IRQ, SCSI_ID, RECONNECT, PARITY, SYNC, DELAY, EXT_TRANS
  IO={0x140,[0x340]}
  IRQ={9,10,[11],12}
  SCSI_ID={0..[7]}
  RECONNECT={0,[1]}
  PARITY={0,[1]}

SYNC={[0],1}

DELAY={..,[100],..}

EXT_TRANS={[0],1}

- possible insmod parameters:

  aha152x=IO, IRQ, SCSI_ID, RECONNECT, PARITY, SYNC, DELAY, EXT_TRANS

  aha152x1=IO, IRQ, SCSI_ID, RECONNECT, PARITY, SYNC, DELAY, EXT_TRANS

  (The meaning and value of items in insmod parameters are given above under boot parameters for this device.)

- devices supported:

  Adaptec 152x, 151x, 1505, 282x, Sound Blaster 16 SCSI, SCSI Pro, Gigabyte, and other AIC 6260/6360 based products (Standard)

Adaptec 154x, AMI FastDisk VLB, DTC 329x (Standard)

- type: scsi (6)
- kernel module: aha1542
- boot parameters: aha1542=IO[,BUSON,BUSOFF[,DMASPEED]]

  IO={0x130,0x134,0x230,0x234,[0x330],0x334,0x340}

  BUSON={2,..,[7],..,15}

  BUSOFF={1,..,[5],..,64}

  DMASPEED={[5],6,7,8,10}
- possible insmod parameters: *none*

Adaptec AHA1740

- type: scsi (7)
- kernel module: aha1740
- boot parameters: *none*
- possible insmod parameters:

  slot=

base=
irq_level={9,10,11,12,14,15}

Adaptec AHA274X/284X/294X

- type: scsi (8)
- kernel module: aic7xxx
- boot parameters: aic7xxx=extended,no_reset,irq_trigger
  extended={0,[1]}   0=extended translation off
- possible insmod parameters:
  aic7xxx_extended={0,1}
  aic7xxx_no_reset={0,1}
  aic7xxx_irq_trigger={-1,0,1}
     -1=use board setting, 0=use edge triggered, 1=use level triggered

Future Domain 16xx

- type: scsi (9)
- kernel module: fdomain
- boot parameters: fdomain=IO,IRQ[,ADAPTER_ID]
- insmod_params:
  port_base={0x140,0x150,0x160,0x170}
  bios_base={0xc8000,0xca000,0xce000,0xde000,0xcc000,0xd0000,0xe0000}
  interrupt_level={3,5,10,11,12,14,15}
  this_id=
- devices supported:
  Future Domain BIOS versions supported for autodetect: 2.0, 3.0, 3.2, 3.4 (1.0), 3.5 (2.0), 3.6, 3.61
  Chips supported: TMC-1800, TMC-18C50, TMC-18C30, TMC-36C70
  Boards supported: Future Domain TMC-1650, TMC-1660, TMC-1670, TMC-1680, TMC-1610M/MER/MEX

Future Domain TMC-3260 (PCI)

Quantum ISA-200S, ISA-250MG

Adaptec AHA-2920 (PCI)

Possibly some IBM boards

Always IN2000

- type: scsi (10)
- kernel module: in2000
- boot parameters: in2000=ioport:addr,noreset,nosync:x,period:ns,disconnect:x,debug:x,proc:x
- possible insmod parameters:

  setup_strings=

  io_ports={0x100,0x110,0x200,0x220}

  irq={10,11,14,15}

  addr={0xc8000,0xd0000,0xd8000}

Generic NCR5380/53c400 SCSI

- type: scsi (11)
- kernel module: g_NCR5380
- boot_param: ncr5380=IO,PORT[,DMA] ncr53c400=IO,IRQ

  IO={[0x350],?}

  IRQ={[5],...,254,255}

  254autoprobe

  255no irq
- possible insmod parameters:

  ncr_addr=IOthe port or base address (for port or memory mapped)

  ncr_irq=IRQthe interrupt

  ncr_dma=DMAthe DMA

  ncr_5380=1to set up for a NCR5380 board

  ncr_53c400=1to set up for a NCR53C400 board

NCR53c406a

- type: scsi (12)
- kernel module: NCR53c406a
- boot parameters: ncr53c406a=IO[,IRQ[,FAST_PIO]]
  IO={0x230,[0x330]}
  IRQ={10,11,12,15}
  FAST_PIO={0,[1]}0: slow 1: fast
- possible insmod parameters:
  port_base=IO
  irq_level=IRQ
  fast_pio=FAST_PIO
  dma_chan={[5],?}
  bios_base={0xD8000,0xc8000}

Qlogicfas Driver version 0.45, chip ... at ..., IRQ ..., TPdma:

- type: scsi (13)
- kernel module: qlogicfas
- boot parameters:*none*
- possible insmod parameters: *none*
- io_ports:
  0x230,0x330

QLogic ISP1020 Intelligent SCSI Processor Driver (PCI)

- type: scsi (14)
- kernel module: qlogicisp
- boot parameters: *none*
- possible insmod parameters: *none*

Pro Audio Spektrum Studio 16

- type: scsi (15)

- kernel module: pas16
- boot parameters: pas16=IO,IRQ
- possible insmod parameters:
  io_port={0x388,0x384,0x38c,0x288}
  irq={3,5,7,10,12,14,15,255}   255=no irq
  noauto=?

Seagate ST0x/Future Domain TMC-8xx/TMC-9xx

- type: scsi (16)
- kernel module: seagate
- boot parameters: st0x=ADR,IRQ tmc8xx=ADR,IRQ
- possible insmod parameters:
  controller_type={1,2}   1=SEAGATE, 2=FD
  base_address={0xc8000,0xca000,0xcc000,0xce000,0xdc000,0xde000}
  irq={3,[5]}

Trantor T128/T128F/T228

- type: scsi (17)
- kernel module: t128
- boot parameters: t128=ADR,IRQ
  ADR={0xcc000,0xc8000,0xdc000,0xd8000}
  IRQ={3,[5],7,10,12,14,15,-1-2}   -1=no irq, -2=autoprobe
- possible insmod parameters:
  address=ADR
  irq=IRQ

DTC 3180/3280

- type: scsi (18)
- kernel module: dtc
- boot parameters: dtc=ADR,IRQ
- posible insmod parameters: *none*

NCR53c{7,8}xx (rel 17)

- type: scsi (19)
- kernel module: 53c7,8xx
- boot parameters:

  ncr53c700,ncr53c700-66,ncr53c710,ncr53c720=mem,io,irq,dma

  ncr53c810,ncr53c820,ncr53c825=mem,io,irq *or* pci,bus,device,function

- possible insmod parameters:

  base=ADR

  io_port=IO

  irq=IRQ

  dma=DMA

  perm_options=BITMASK

      where BITMASK is "logical or" of the following flags

OPTION_SYNCHRONOUS	0x400
OPTION_IO_MAPPED	0x1000
OPTION_DEBUG_TEST1	0x10000
OPTION_DISCONNECT	0x8000000
OPTION_ALWAYS_SYNCHRONOUS	0x20000000

     so

normal	0x11400
disconnect	0x8011400
sync	0x20011400
sync & disconnect	0x28011400

NCR 53C810, 53C815, 53C820, 53C825

- type: scsi (20)
- kernel module: ncr53c8xx
- boot parameters: *none*
- possible insmod parameters: *none*
- devices supported:

NCR 53C810, 53C815, 53C820, 53C825

EATA-DMA (DPT, NEC, AT&T, SNI, AST, Olivetti, Alphatronix)

- type: scsi (21)
- kernel module: eata_dma
- boot parameters:
- possible insmod parameters:
- io_ports:
  0x1F0,0x170,0x330,0x230 (ISA)
  0x1c88 (in 0x1000 steps) (EISA)
- devices supported:
  ISA based EATA-DMA boards like PM2011, PM2021, PM2041, PM3021
  EISA based EATA-DMA boards like PM2012B, PM2022, PM2122, PM2322, PM2042, PM3122, PM3222, PM3332
  PCI based EATA-DMA boards like PM2024, PM2124, PM2044, PM2144, PM3224, PM3334

EATA-PIO (old DPT PM2001, PM2012A)

- type: scsi (22)
- kernel module: eata_pio
- boot parameter:
- possible insmod parameters:
- io_ports:
  0x1F0,0x170,0x330,0x230

Western Digital WD 7000 (FASST/ASC/xX)

- type: scsi (23)
- kernel module: wd7000
- boot parameters: wd7000=IRQ,DMA
- possible insmod parameters:

wd7000_setupIRQ=IRQ

wd7000_setupDMA=DMA

- io_ports:
0x300,0x308,0x310,0x318,0x320,0x328,0x330,0x338,
0x340,0x348,0x350,0x358,0x360,0x368,0x370,0x378,
0x380,0x388,0x390,0x398,0x3a0,0x3a8,0x3b0,0x3b8,
0x3c0,0x3c8,0x3d0,0x3d8,0x3e0,0x3e8,0x3f0,0x3f8

EATA ISA/EISA (DPT PM2011/021/012/022/122/322)

- type: scsi (24)
- kernel module: eata
- boot parameters:
- possible insmod parameters:
- devices supported:
DPT SmartCache, SmartCache Plus, SmartCache III, SmartCache IV
and SmartRAID (Standard)

AM53C974

- type: scsi (25)
- kernel module: -

- boot parameters: AM53C974=HOST_SCSI_ID,
TARGET_SCSI_ID, MAX_RATE, MAX_OFFSET

HOST_SCSI_ID?	SCSI id of the bus controller
TARGET_SCSI_ID?	SCSI id of target
MAX_RATE?	max. transfer rate
MAX_OFFSET?	max. sync. offset (0=asynchronous)

- possible insmod parameters:
- devices supported:
AM53/79C974 PCI SCSI

ppa

- type: scsi (26)
- kernel module: ppa
- boot parameters: ppa=IO[,SPEED_HIGH[,SPEED_LOW[,NYBBLE]]]

IO0x378	The base address of PPA's parallel port
SPEED_HIGH	1 Microsecond i/o delay used in data transfers
SPEED_LOW	6 Microsecond delay used in other operations
NYBBLE	01 to force the driver to use 4-bit mode

- possible insmod parameters:

ppa_base=IO0x378	The base address of PPA's parallel port
ppa_speed_high=MS	1 Microsecond i/o delay used in data transfers
ppa_speed_low=MS	6 Microsecond delay used in other operations
ppa_nybble=N	01 to force the driver to use 4-bit mode

- devices supported:

  IOMEGA Parallel Port ZIP drive

Network Card Parameters

Most network cards accept the following boot parameters:

    ether=IRQ,IO,MEM_START,MEM_END,DEV_NAME

Most network cards accept the following insmod parameters:

    io=IO
    irq=IRQ

Other Parameters

There are many other parameters that are not specific to certain vendors' hardware, as the parameters given above are. Information about these other parameters is included in two Linux HOWTO documents—the BootPrompt HOWTO and the Modules HOWTO. These documents can be viewed from the Caldera Info icon on your Desktop, under Linux references, or on the Caldera Web site under Linux References.

Configuring the X Window System

After you install Caldera's OpenLinux Base, you can configure the X Window System. Base gives you two different X Window servers to choose from: Metro-X and XFree86.

This chapter explains how to do these tasks:

- Configure XFree86.
- Start the X Window System.
- Toggle between screen resolutions.

Configuring XFree86

To use XFree86, you must first install the correct X server package for the video hardware. If the correct X server isn't found, the configuration utility will let you know.

This section explains how to do these tasks:

- Start the configuration.

- Configure the mouse.
- Configure the keyboard.
- Configure the video card.
- Configure the monitor.
- Configure other settings.
- Adjust the display settings.

Starting the Configuration

1. Log in as root.

2. **Enter this command:** /usr/X11R6/bin/XF86Setup. A configuration file is created at this location on your hard disk: /etc/XF86Config, then you're asked to enter graphics mode.

3. **Choose "Yes," then press** ENTER **to enter graphics mode.**

Configuring the Mouse

NOTE: Do not use your mouse until after you've configured it; otherwise, problems may occur.

1. **Choose the Mouse button (or press** ALT+M**).** Instructions for configuring the system appear.

2. **Press** ENTER **to continue.** The mouse configuration screen appears.

3. **Complete these settings:**

To set the double-click speed of your mouse, use the ↓ (down arrow) and ↑ (up arrow) keys.

To set the minutes before a timeout, use the ↓ (down arrow) and ↑ (up arrow) keys.

Choose the brand of your mouse.

Choose the mouse device path, or enter

Choose the number of buttons on your mouse.

Choose the baud rate of your mouse.

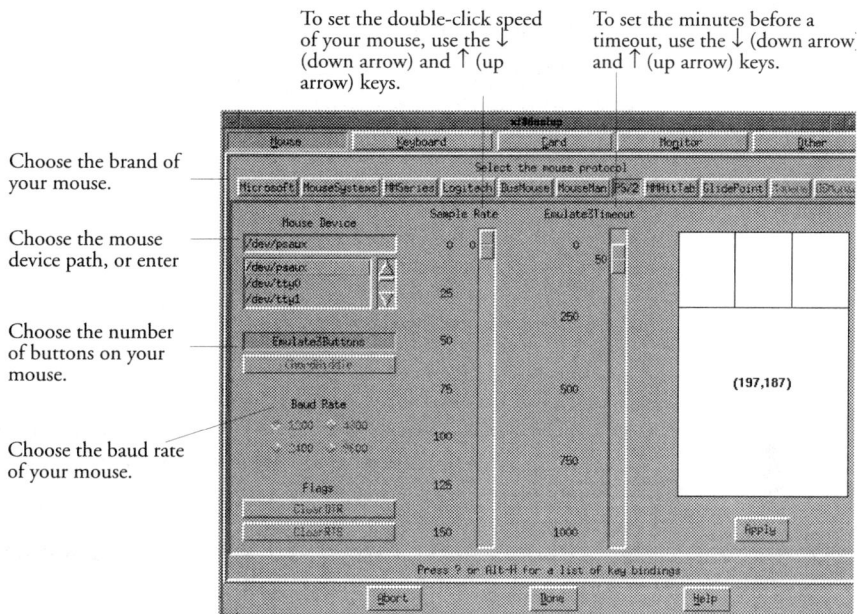

FIGURE 1. Configuring the mouse settings

4. **Choose the Apply button.** You can now use the mouse to configure the rest of the system.

5. **If you're done configuring XFree, use this table; otherwise, continue with the next task.**

When you're done configuring XFree
a. Click on the Done button. You're asked if you're done configuring the X server.
b. Click on the Okay button. After a few moments, you're prompted to run xvidtune or save the configuration.
c. To adjust the display settings, see the next task; otherwise, click on "Save the configuration and exit."

TABLE 9. Leaving the X configuration

Configuring the Keyboard

1. **Choose the Keyboard button.** The keyboard configuration screen appears.

2. **Complete these settings:**

If necessary, choose any of these system behaviors.

If necessary, choose any of these control key positions.

Choose the keyboard model (usually Generic).

Choose the keyboard language.

If you choose a non-U.S. keyboard, choose a variant.

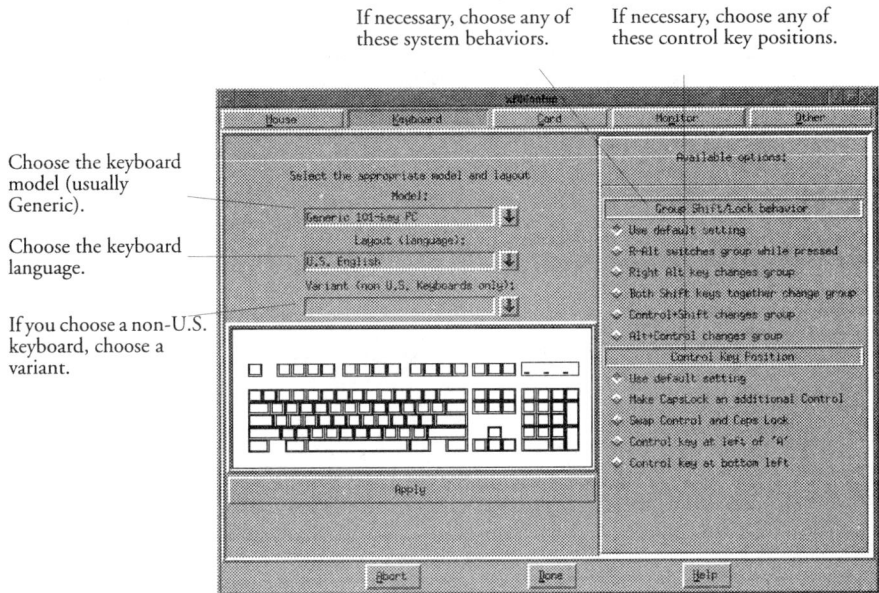

FIGURE 2. **Configuring the keyboard**

3. **Choose the Apply button to apply these settings immediately.**

4. If you're done configuring XFree, use this table; otherwise, continue with the next task:

When you're done configuring XFree
a. Click on the Done button. You're asked if you're done configuring the X server.
b. Click on the Okay button. After a few moments, you're prompted to run xvidtune or save the configuration.
c. To adjust the display settings, see the next task; otherwise, click on "Save the configuration and exit."

TABLE 10. Leaving the X configuration

Configuring the Video Card

1. Choose the Card button.

2. Choose your system's video card from the list:

The video card you chose.

List of video cards.

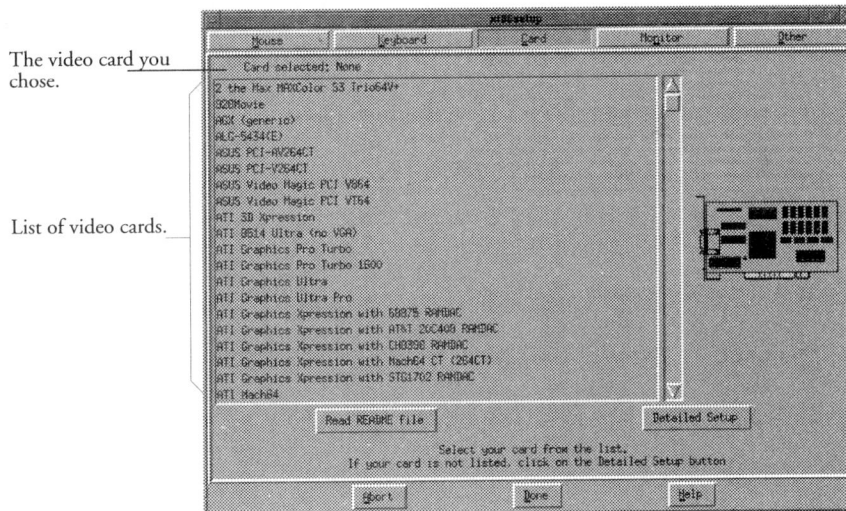

FIGURE 3. Choosing a video card

The video card settings are complete.

NOTE: If your system's video card isn't listed, choose the Detailed Setup button, then complete the applicable fields.

3.   **If you're done configuring XFree, use this table; otherwise, continue with the next task:**

When you're done configuring XFree
a. Click on the Done button. You're asked if you're done configuring the X server.
b. Click on the Okay button. After a few moments, you're prompted to run xvidtune or save the configuration.
c. To adjust the display settings, see the next task; otherwise, click on "Save the configuration and exit."

TABLE 11. Leaving the X configuration

Configuring the Monitor

WARNING: Before you choose a monitor frequency (Hz), check your hardware documentation. If your monitor doesn't support a frequency as high as one you select, your monitor may be damaged.

1.   Choose the Monitor button.

2.   Do one of these:

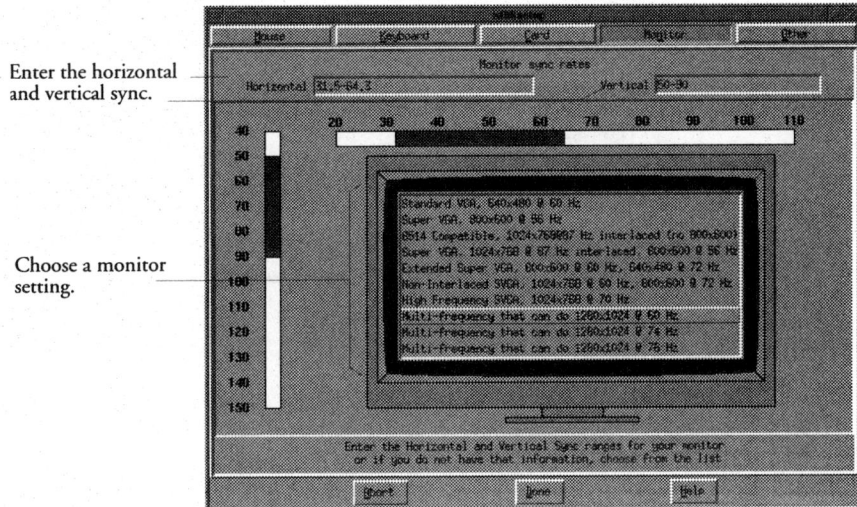

Enter the horizontal and vertical sync.

Choose a monitor setting.

FIGURE 4. Configuring the monitor

3. If you're done configuring XFree, use this table; otherwise, continue with the next task:

When you're done configuring XFree
a. Click on the Done button. You're asked if you're done configuring the X server.
b. Click on the Okay button. After a few moments, you're prompted to run xvidtune or save the configuration.
c. To adjust the display settings, see the next task; otherwise, click on "Save the configuration and exit."

TABLE 12. Leaving the X configuration

Configuring Other Settings

If you want to configure your system with other settings, do this task (for example, you can set up video mode switching).

1. If necessary, choose the Other button.

2. Choose any of these options:

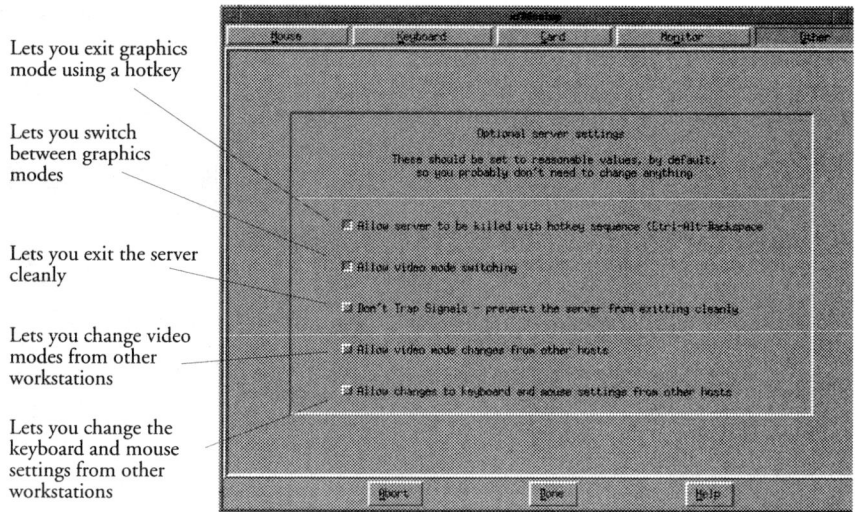

Lets you exit graphics mode using a hotkey

Lets you switch between graphics modes

Lets you exit the server cleanly

Lets you change video modes from other workstations

Lets you change the keyboard and mouse settings from other workstations

FIGURE 5. **Other system settings**

3. If you're done configuring XFree, use this table:

When you're done configuring Xfree
a. Click on the Done button. You're asked if you're done configuring the X server.
b. Click on the Okay button. After a few moments, you're prompted to run xvidtune or save the configuration.
c. To adjust the display settings, see the next task; otherwise, click on "Save the configuration and exit."

TABLE 13. Leaving the X configuration

Adjusting the Display Settings

After you configure XFree, you can adjust the settings of your display area. For example, you can change the width and height of your display area, or move the display area to the left or right.

1. **If you're prompted to adjust the display settings, click on the Run xvidtune button.** A warning message appears. If you aren't familiar with xvidtune, click Cancel to end this task.

   Note: You can adjust the display settings at any time by entering xvidtune from a command line.

2. **Click on the OK button to continue.**

3. **Configure the display:**

Click these buttons to move the display area to the left or right.

Click these buttons to make the display area wider or narrower.

Click these buttons to move the display area up or down.

Click these button make the display a shorter or taller.

4. **When you've made the necessary adjustments, click the Apply button.** Your changes are displayed. Repeat step 3 until your settings are correct.

5. **To save your changes, click on the Quit button; otherwise, click on the Restore button, then click on the Quit button.**

6. **Click the Okay button to complete the configuration.** You're now ready to start using the X Window System.

Starting the X Window System

After you've configured the X Window System, you're ready to use it. When you start the X Window System, the Caldera graphical desktop also appears. To start X and the graphical system, enter startx.

Toggling Between Screen Resolutions

Once you've configured the X Window System, you can switch between the resolutions you selected.

1. If your haven't already, log in and enter startx to start the graphical system.

2. Do one to select the screen resolution you want:

    *   Press CTRL+ALT++ (plus on 10-key pad) for the next screen resolution.
    *   Press CTRL+ALT+- (minus on 10-key pad) for the previous screen resolution.

APPENDIX B *Software Packages Index*

The Caldera OpenLinux Lite CD-ROM included with this book contains nearly 700 MB of compressed software. The software is divided into packages based on its function. For example, one software package contains the Desktop interface and related components, another package contains the Apache World Wide Web server, and another contains the CRiSPlite editor.

You determined what packages are on your system by the Installation option you selected while installing OpenLinux.You can install additional packages from the CD-ROM or from another location, such as a hard disk archive of the CD-ROM, or the Caldera FTP site. Each software package can be installed or uninstalled with a single command. For instructions on installing and removing packages, see page 64. All package names are *case sensitive*.

This Appendix lists all of the packages that are on the CD-ROM. Software packages that are Caldera-Proprietary (and therefore cannot be freely-distributed) are marked with an asterisk (*). Some other packages that are not marked in the table are also distributed by Caldera under special arrangement with the copyright holder, and may not be commercially redistributed without permission from the copyright holder.

If you need to locate a specific file or software package, you can also refer to the online index of files on the CD-ROM, in the /col/data directory.

TABLE 14. Software packages on the Caldera OpenLinux Lite CD-ROM

Package	Description
*COL	Caldera Open Linux setup files.
*COLbaseCD-doc	Caldera Open Linux setup files.
*CRiSPlite	CRiSPlite Editor for Linux.
*CRiSPlite-doc	The CRiSPlite Editor User's Manual.
DEV	All necessary block and character devices for Linux.
ElectricFence	Development library for the kernel malloc debugger.
ImageMagick	Graphics package for displaying, converting and manipulating various image formats under X.
ImageMagick-devel	Static libraries and header files for development of graphical applications based on ImageMagick.
LPRng	Enhanced replacement for the standard UNIX printing tools.
LPRng-lpd	Enhanced UNIX print daemon compatible with the lpr standard.
LSM	The Linux Software Map.
NetKit-B	Various network programs.
SysVinit	System V compatible INIT program.
SysVinit-scripts	Scripts for System V init, such as 'inittab' and '/etc/rc.d'.
XFree86	XFree86 window system servers and fundamental programs.
XFree86-8514	XFree86 8514 server.

TABLE 14. Software packages on the Caldera OpenLinux Lite CD-ROM

Package	Description
XFree86-AGX	XFree86 AGX server.
XFree86-I128	XFree86 I128 server.
XFree86-Mach32	XFree86 Mach32 server.
XFree86-Mach64	XFree86 Mach64 server.
XFree86-Mach8	XFree86 Mach8 server.
XFree86-Mono	XFree86 Mono server.
XFree86-P9000	XFree86 P9000 server.
XFree86-S3	XFree86 S3 server.
XFree86-S3V	XFree86 S3 ViRGE and ViRGE/VX server.
XFree86-SVGA	XFree86 SVGA server.
XFree86-VGA16	XFree86 VGA16 server.
XFree86-W32	XFree86 W32 server.
XFree86-Xnest	XFree86 nesting server.
XFree86-Xvfb	XFree86 Xvfb server.
XFree86-addons	X11R6 miscelleanous programs and their man pages.
XFree86-contrib	Additional programs for X11R6 from the 'contrib tapes'.
XFree86-devel	X11R6 static libraries, headers and programming man pages.
XFree86-develprof	X11R6 profiling libraries.
XFree86-develstatic	X11R6 static libraries.
XFree86-fonts	XFree86 Window System basic fonts.
XFree86-fonts100	X11R6 100dpi fonts.
XFree86-fonts75	X11R6 75dpi fonts.

TABLE 14. Software packages on the Caldera OpenLinux Lite CD-ROM

Package	Description
XFree86-fontscyrillic	X11R6 cyrillic fonts - only need on server side.
XFree86-fontserver	X11R6 font server - only needed on server side.
XFree86-fontsextra	X11R6 hebrew and asiatic fonts - only needed on server side.
XFree86-fontsscale	X11R6 scalable fonts - only needed on server side.
XFree86-imake	X11R6 'imake' programming tools.
XFree86-misc	X11R6 miscelleanous programs and their man pages.
XFree86-programs	Additional programs for X11R6 from the 'contrib tapes'.
XFree86-server	XFree86 Window System server basic stuff.
XFree86-server-devel	XFree86 devel stuff for dga, misc, vidmode.
XFree86-server-modules	XFree86 loadable server modules for pex, xie, dga
XFree86-setup	XFree86 setup program 'XF86Setup'.
XFree86-twm	Tab window manager for X.
XFree86-xdm	Display manager allowing the user to log in or out of the system under X.
XFree86-xsm	X session manager.
Xaw3d	The 3D Athena widget libraries version 1.3, which can replace the normal Athena widget library.
Xaw3d-devel	Header files and static libraries for developing programs that use Xaw3d.
Xconfigurator	X configuration utility.
abuse	Abuse - A really cool X/SVGA game.
acm	X based flight combat game.
adduser	User administration program.
adjtimex	User level frontend to adjtimex-syscall.

TABLE 14. Software packages on the Caldera OpenLinux Lite CD-ROM

Package	Description
amd	The auto mounter which allows filesystemsto be mounted on demand.
anonftp	Enables anonymous ftp access.
aout-libs	Libraries for compatibility with old a.out applications.
apache-docs	Documentation for the apache HTTP server.
apache-httpd	Apache HTTP server to provide WWW services.
archie	Information retrival system to query special archie databases containing entries from various FTP sites all over the net.
arena	Freely available, HTML-3 capable, WWW browser.
ash	Small bourne shell from Berkeley (only 40k).
at	The 'at' command allows processes to be started at a predetermined time.
aumix	Curses based audio mixer.
autoconf	Extendable package of GNU m4 macros which creates shell scripts to automatically configure source code packages. This package requires the GNU 'm4' package.
background	Additional background pictures for the X desktop.
bash	The GNU Bourne Again Shell which is functionally comparable to 'tcsh' and is the standard shell under Linux.
bc	GNU binary calculator with its own calculator language.
bdflush	The kernel daemon 'bdflush' is used to write altered data blocks in the cache back to the harddisk at regular intervals. This replaces the old update daemon.

TABLE 14. Software packages on the Caldera OpenLinux Lite CD-ROM

Package	Description
bin86	The assembler 'as86', linker 'ld86', and GCC frontend 'bcc' from H.J. Lu.
bind	DNS name server used for name services in networks.
bind-lib	DNS resolver library and headers.
bind-utils	DNS utilities, e.g. 'host', 'dig', 'dnsquery', 'nslookup'.
binutils	GNU binary development utilities.
bison	GNU parser generator (mighter than 'yacc').
blt	More widgets for the tk widget set.
blt-devel	Development libraries and header files for the BLT widgets.
bm2font	Bm2font converts bitmaps to LaTeX fonts.
bootp	Bootp/DHCP server that allows clients to automatically get their networking information.
bootpc	Bootpc, a client to get networking info from bootpd.
bsd-games	The BSD game collection contains classic games like 'backgammon', 'cribbage', 'fortune', 'hangman' and 'worms'.
buffer	Utility to speed up writing tapes on remote tape drives.
byacc	Public domain yacc parser generator.
cdp	Full screen text mode program for playing audio CD's.
cdwrite	Writes audio or data Compact Discs.
cmu-snmp	CMU Simple Network Management Protocol agent.
cmu-snmp-devel	CMU SNMP development libs and headers.

TABLE 14. Software packages on the Caldera OpenLinux Lite CD-ROM

Package	Description
cmu-snmp-utils	CMU Simple Network Management Protocol utilities.
color-ls	Color ls - patched from GNU fileutils.
control-panel	Red Hat Control Panel.
coolmail	Shows status of the mailbox.
cpio	GNU 'cpio' archiving program (used by rpm).
cproto	C prototype utility.
crontabs	Root crontab file.
cvs	Concurrent version control system, a comprehensive frontend to 'rcs', the GNU revision control system. 'cvs' also operates on directory trees.
cxhextris	X based color version of hextris.
db	BSD database library for C.
db-devel	Development libraries and header files for the Berkeley database library.
ddd-doc	Motif based X interface to the GDB, DBX and XDB debuggers. Documentation and manual page
ddd-dynamic	Motif based X interface to the GDB, DBX and XDB debuggers. Uses Motif 2.0 shared libraries
ddd-semistatic	Motif based X interface to the GDB, DBX and XDB debuggers. With Motif 2.0 libraries statically linked in
ddd-static	Motif based X interface to the GDB, DBX and XDB debuggers. Completely statically linked
dialog	Tool to display tty dialog boxes from shell scripts.
diffutils	GNU 'diff' utilities differentiate files.

TABLE 14. Software packages on the Caldera OpenLinux Lite CD-ROM

Package	Description
dip	Dip allows automatic modem dialing and creation of IP connections to be controlled with a script language.
dosemu	The experimental DOS emulator.
dthelp	Online help for the Caldera Looking Glass desktop.
dump	BSD dump/restore backup system for extended-2 filesystems.
e2fsprogs	Programs and utilities for the extended-2 filesystem.
e2fsprogs-devel	Libraries and headers for the extended-2 filesystem tools.
easyedit	The 'easyedit' extension for Emacs.
ecc	Reed-Solomon Error Correcting Coder.
ed	GNU Line Editor 'ed', an 8-bit-clean POSIX line editor.
edy	Edy, a German coloured, window based editor.
efax	Sends and receives faxes over class 1 or class 2 modems.
eject	Ejects ejectable media and controls auto ejection.
elm	Menu based mail program 'elm'.
elvis	Elvis editor (Elvis is like VI).
exmh	'exmh' mail program.
expect	A 'tcl' extension that allows easy interaction between programs and scripts.
expect-devel	The development and demo part of expect with man-pages
ext2ed	Extended-2 filesystem editor (*for hackers only*).
f2c	Fortran to C convertor and static libraries.

TABLE 14. Software packages on the Caldera OpenLinux Lite CD-ROM

Package	Description
f2c-libs	Shared libs for running dynamically linked fortran programs.
faces	Face saver database tools.
faces-devel	Face saver library and header.
faces-xface	Utilities to handle X-Face headers.
faq	FAQs - Frequently Asked Questions and answers about Linux.
fdutils	Low level floppy disk programs.
file	The GNU 'file' utility determines the type of any file with the help of '/etc/magic'.
fileutils	GNU File Utilities, a collection of many fundamental Unix programs.
findutils	GNU search utilities (find, xargs, and locate).
flex	GNU fast lexical analyzer generator.
flying	Pool, snooker, air hockey, and other table games.
fort77	A frontend driver for 'f2c'.
fortune-mod	Fortune cookie program with bug fixes.
free-lj4	Remote control tool for HP LJ4 printer series.
free-lj4-german	Remote control tool for HP LJ4 printer series in German.
fsstnd	Linux File System Standard documentation.
fstool	File system configuration tools.
ftptool	A nice ftp front end under Xview.
fvwm	Feeble (Fine?) Virtual Window Manager (incl. menus and configuration files).
fvwm-icons	Additional icons for the 'fvwm' window manager.

TABLE 14. Software packages on the Caldera OpenLinux Lite CD-ROM

Package	Description
fvwm-modules	Additional modules for the fvwm window manager.
fwhois	A 'finger' style whois tool.
g77	GNU Fortran compiler 'g77'.
g77_lib	GNU Fortran 'g77' library
gawk	GNU 'awk' utility for manipulating patterns in text files.
gcal	Extended calendar with highlighting, holidays, etc.
gcc	GNU 'gcc' C compiler.
gcc-c++	C++ support for 'gcc'.
gcc-objc	Objective C support for 'gcc'.
gdb	GNU 'gdb', symbolic debugger for C and other languages.
gdbm	GNU database library for C.
gdbm-devel	Development libraries and header files for GNU database library.
gdbm-static	'gdbm libraries for static linking.
gencat	'gencat' message cataloging program (from NetBSD).
german-docs-L-Kurs	L-Kurs - An Introduction to Linux in German.
german-docs-intro	Linux documentation in German.
gettext	Utilties and libraries for programming with national language support (NLS).
getty_ps	Getty and uugetty programs for logging in.
ghostscript	PostScript interpreter and renderer.
ghostscript-fonts	Fonts for GhostScript.
ghostview	Ghostview user interface for ghostscript.

TABLE 14. Software packages on the Caldera OpenLinux Lite CD-ROM

Package	Description
giftrans	Converts and manipulates GIFs.
gimp-static	General Image Manipulation Program, a Photoshop-like tool with many plug-ins.
git	GIT - GNU Interactive Tools.
glint	Graphical Linux INstallation Tool
gn	Gopher server.
gnat	GNU Ada compiler.
gnuchess	GNU 'chess' with 'xboard'. GNU Chess is a challenging ASCII based chess program and XBoard is its X interface.
gnuplot	'gnuplot', an interactive tool for displaying values and functions.
gpm	General purpose mouse support for Linux.
gpm-devel	Development libraries and headers for writing mouse driven programs.
grep	GNU 'grep' utility.
groff	GNU 'groff' text formating utility.
groff-dvi	GNU 'groff' formatter for DVI.
groff-gxditview	GNU 'groff' formatter for preview under X.
groff-lj4	GNU 'groff' formatter for HP Laserjet 4 printers.
groff-misc	GNU 'groff' miscelleanous tools.
groff-ps	GNU 'groff' formatter for Postscript.
gzip	GNU 'gzip' compression utility version 1.2.4.
hdparm	Harddisk utility for reading and setting (E)IDE performance parameters
helptool	Simple help file searching tool.

TABLE 14. Software packages on the Caldera OpenLinux Lite CD-ROM

Package	Description
hman	Motif based manual browser under X.
howto-ascii	Linux HOWTO documents in ascii format.
howto-dvi	Linux HOWTO documents in dvi format.
howto-html	Linux HOWTO documents in html format.
howto-ps	Linux HOWTO documents in postscript format.
howto-sgml	Linux HOWTO documents in sgml format.
html	Hyper text markup language 3.0 documentation in html format.
iBCS	Intel binary compliance standard (iBCS-2) module.
ical	Calender application based on Tcl/Tk.
illustrated-audio	Combined image and sound player for X.
imap	Provides support for IMAP and POP network mail protocols.
indent	GNU C indenting program for formatting C source code.
inn	'internetnews' news transport system.
intimed	Time server for clock synchornization.
ipfwadm	IP firewall administration tool.
ipx	Utilites, init scripts, man pages and configuration files for IPX (Internetwork Packet Exchange - a Novell-centric datagram protocol).
ipxripd	IPX RIP/SAP daemon for discovering/advertising IPX routing information (RIP) and services (SAP) across an IPX internetwork.
ircii	Popular Unix Internet Relay Chat client.
ircii-help	Help files and documentation for ircii.

TABLE 14. Software packages on the Caldera OpenLinux Lite CD-ROM

Package	Description
isdn4k-utils	Utilities for the kernel ISDN subsystem and some contributions.
ispell	GNU ispell - interactive spelling checker.
jed	Editor with multiple, keybindings, a c-like extension language, colors, and many other features.
jed-xjed	Jed editor for X.
joe	Joe, the easy to use editor.
kbd	The loadable keyboard driver 'kbd'. Required for loading alternative keyboard layouts.
koules	A well written SVGAlib game.
kterm	Xterm with Kanji (japanese characters) support.
ktzset	Sets kernel time zone at boot time.
ld.so	'ld.so' dynamic linker for shared libraries. With ancilliary programs. Contains 'ldconfig' and 'ldd' as well.
ldp-dvi	Linux Documentation Project in dvi format.
ldp-ps	Linux Documentation Project in postscript format.
ldp-txt	Linux Documentation Project in ascii format.
less	The pager 'less'.
*lg	Caldera Looking Glass desktop.
*lg-doc	Caldera Desktop User's Guide.
*lg-pg	Caldera Desktop Program Groups.
*lg-rules	Caldera Desktop File Typing Rules and Layouts.
lha	Creates and expands lharc format archives.
libc	Libc and related libraries.
libc-debug	Libc with debugging information.

TABLE 14. Software packages on the Caldera OpenLinux Lite CD-ROM

Package	Description
libc-devel	Additional, for compiling essential libraries.
libc-profile	Libc with profiling support.
libc-static	Libraries for static linking.
libelf	Library for manipulating ELF object files.
libg++	GNU 'g++' library.
libg++-devel	Header files and libraries for C++ development.
libgnat	Ada run time system and shared library.
libgr	Graphics library set for fbm, jpeg, pbm, pgm, png, pnm, ppm, rle and tiff.
libgr-devel	Headers and static libraries for developing graphical applications.
libgr-progs	Utility programs for libgr.
libpam	PAM (pluggable authentication modules), a library for dynamic (re)configuration of user authentication methods like /etc/passwd, /etc/shadow, S/key and kerberos.
libpwdb	modular password database library
libtermcap	Library for accessing the termcap database.
libtermcap-devel	Development libraries and header files for termcap library.
libtiff-develdoc	Additional man pages for the functions in libtiff.
lilo	'LILO', the boot loader for Linux and other operating systems from Werner Almesberger.
linux-kernel-binary	Linux kernel image and modules.
linux-kernel-doc	Linux kernel documentation.
linux-kernel-include	Linux kernel include files (required for C programming)

TABLE 14. **Software packages on the Caldera OpenLinux Lite CD-ROM**

Package	Description
linux-source-alpha	Linux kernel sources for alpha axp architecture
linux-source-common	Linux kernel sources (architecture independent common sources).
linux-source-i386	Linux kernel sources for intel i386 architecture.
linux-source-m68k	Linux kernel sources for motorola m68k architecture.
linux-source-mips	Linux kernel sources for mips architecture.
linux-source-ppc	Linux kernel sources for power pc architecture
linux-source-sparc	Linux kernel sources for sparc architecture.
linuxdoc-sgml	Text formatting system used by the Linux Documentation Project.
*lisa	Linux Installation and System Administration Utility.
logrotate	Log file rotator.
losetup	Programs for setting up and configuring loopback devices.
lout	'lout' text formatting system.
lout-doc	Full documentation for the 'lout' text formatting system.
lrzsz	Zmodem programs such as 'lzrz', 'sz', 'rz' and others.
lynx	Ascii based HTML browser.
lyx	A WYSIWYG frontend to LaTeX.
m4	GNU 'm4' macro processor.
macutils	Utilities for manipulating Macintosh file formats.
mailcap	Red Hat Mailcap package.
mailx	BSD 'mailx' mail program.
make	The GNU 'make' utility.

TABLE 14. Software packages on the Caldera OpenLinux Lite CD-ROM

Package	Description
man-pages	System manual pages from the Linux Documentation Project.
man_db	Manual page reader.
maplay	Plays MPEG-2 audio files in 16 bit stereo.
mawk	Mike's New/Posix AWK Interpreter.
mc	Midnight Commander visual shell.
metamail	Tools and programs for multimedia email.
mgetty	Smart getty replacement for data and fax modems.
mh	'mh' mail handling system, with POP support, for use with 'xmh'.
minicom	Minicom, a TTY mode communications package with support for European characters.
mkdosfs-ygg	Creates a DOS FAT filesystem.
mkisofs	Creates a ISO9660 filesystem image, also with Rock-Ridge extensions.
ml	Motif based mail handling programm, supporting pop3d news reading, MIME etc.
modemtool	Configuration tool for /dev/modem.
modules	Utilities for the loadable Linux kernel modules by Bjorn Ekwall and Jaques Gelinas.
moonclock	Traditional oclock with moon phase hacks.
mount	Programs for mounting and unmounting filesystems.
moxfm	Moxfm is a full-fledged file and application manager.
mpage	Places multiple pages of text onto a single postscript page for printing.
mpeg_play	X based player for mpeg files including Red's Nightmare demo.

TABLE 14. Software packages on the Caldera OpenLinux Lite CD-ROM

Package	Description
mt-st	The 'mt' tool allows access to streamer tapes.
mtools	'mtools' allows access to DOS filesystems.
multimedia	A CD player and audio mixer for X.
mush	A comfortable interface for electronic mail.
mxp	X mandelbrot set generator and explorer.
ncftp	Ftp client with a nice interface.
ncompress	Extremely fast LZW based file compressor by Peter Jannesen.
ncsa	NCSA HTTP server daemon for providing WWW services.
ncurses	'ncurses' terminal control library.
ncurses-devel	Development libraries for 'ncurses'.
nenscript	Converts plain ascii to PostScript.
net-tools	Basic network tools e.g. ifconfig, route, ...
netcfg	Network configuration tool.
netpbm	Lots of image conversion and manipulation tools (hpcd support is missing due to a very restrictive redistribution clause).
nfs-server	NFS server daemons.
nfs-server-clients	Client applicationss for use with remote NFS servers.
nis-client	Network Information Service client (formerly yp).
nis-server	Network Information Service server (formerly yp).
nls	Native Language Support (NLS) files for Motif, Netscape, etc.
nvi	New Berkeley vi editor (experimental).

TABLE 14. Software packages on the Caldera OpenLinux Lite CD-ROM

Package	Description
open	Tools for creating and switching between virtual consoles.
optprep	For installing third-party rpm packages such as Caldera's Internet Office Suite.
p2c	Shared library for programs built with the 'p2c' Pascal to C convertor
p2c-basic	A BASIC interpreter based on Pascal using the 'p2c' package.
p2c-devel	Programs and headers for the Pascal to C translator.
pam-apps	Pluggable Authentication Modules (PAM) for Linux.
paradise	Enhanced 'netrek' client with sound and color.
patch	GNU patch Utilities.
pcmcia-cs	PCMCIA Card Services. Tool to support 'hot-swapping' of PCMCIA cards.
pdksh	Public domain korn shell.
perf-rstatd	System monitor using rstatd services (included).
perl	PERL, Practical Extraction and Report Language, Larry Wall's interpreted script language.
perl-add	Practical Extraction and Report Language extensions.
perl-eg	Practical Extraction and Report Language examples.
perl-man	Practical Extraction and Report Language man pages.
perl-pod	Practical Extraction and Report Language documentation.
perl4	Practical Extraction and Report Language (old version).
pidentd	Internet Daemon Authorization, User Identification.

TABLE 14. Software packages on the Caldera OpenLinux Lite CD-ROM

Package	Description
pine	MIME compliant mail reader with news support as well.
pixmap	X based, comfortable pixmap editor.
plan	Motif based scheduler/planner.
playmidi	Play MIDI files on FM, GUS and MIDI devices.
pmake	Berkeley's parallel make.
pmirror	'mirror', a perl script for mirroring an FTP site.
popclient	POP - retrieve mail from a mailserver using Post Office Protocol.
portmap	The RPC portmapper daemon.
ppp	'PPP', Point to Point Protocoll.
printtool	Tool for printer configuration under X (Tcl/Tk based).
procinfo	'/proc' filesystem information.
procmail	'procmail', a program to filter and process email.
procps	A collection of programs which evaluate the '/proc' structure of the system ('free', 'top', 'uptime' ...).
procps-X11	X based process monitoring utilities.
project-map	Map of Linux projects in progress.
psmisc	More 'ps' type tools for /proc filesystem.
psutils	PostScript Utilities.
python	Very high level scripting language with X interface.
pythonlib	Library of python code used by various Red Hat programs.
rcs	GNU 'rcs' - revision control system.

TABLE 14. Software packages on the Caldera OpenLinux Lite CD-ROM

Package	Description
rdate	Sets the system clock from a network reference. Accurate to about 1 second.
rdist	Remote file distribution client that allows management of identical copies of files on multiple computers.
readline	Library for reading lines from a terminal.
readline-devel	Libraries and header files for developing programs that use the 'readline' library.
recode	Utility for converting textfiles between different fonts according RFC 1345.
rpm	Red Hat Package Manager.
rpm-devel	Header files and libraries for programs that manipulate rpm packages.
rxvt	'rxvt' - terminal emulator in an X window.
samba	Samba is a Unix based SMB fileserver. It enables a Linux host to become a file and printserver for WfW, OS/2, NT or Windows 95. It also contains a SMB client and a NetBIOS nameserver.
sc	Text based spreadsheet with date support (requires ncurses-devel and bison).
screen	A screen manager with VT100/ANSI emulation, which can be used as a terminal multiplexer operating multiple virtual terminals that can be controlled from one single real terminal.
sed	GNU 'sed' stream editor.
sendmail	Mail transport agent 'sendmail'.
sendmail-cf	'sendmail' configuration files and m4 macros.
sendmail-doc	'sendmail' documentation.
setup	Simple setup files

TABLE 14. Software packages on the Caldera OpenLinux Lite CD-ROM

Package	Description
seyon	'seyon' is a complete X based communication package for modems.
sh-utils	Collection of shell programmers' utilities such as 'basename', 'date', 'dirname', 'expr', 'nohup', 'nice' and 'stty'.
sharutils	GNU shar utils like 'shar', 'unshar', 'uuencode' and 'uudecode'.
slang	Shared library for the C like S-Lang language.
slang-devel	Static library and header files for the C like S-Lang language.
sliplogin	Slip server (derived from BSD 'sliplogin') which works with shadow system and mgetty.
slrn	Small NNTP newsreader.
slsc	Spreadsheet based on 'sc', but with many enhancements.
sox	General purpose sound file conversion tool.
spice	SPICE circuit simulator.
spider	X implementation of the card game Spider.
stat	File information reporter.
statnet	Monitors network traffic in a terminal.
statserial	Displays status of the serial lines in a terminal.
strace	Prints system call trace of a running process.
svgalib	Library for full screen (S)VGA graphics.
svgalib-devel	Development libraries and include files for (S)VGA graphics.
swatch	System log watcher and alarm.
symlinks	Symbolic link sanity checker.

TABLE 14. Software packages on the Caldera OpenLinux Lite CD-ROM

Package	Description
sysklogd	Linux system and kernel logger.
taper	Tape backup system (beta).
tar	GNU tape archiver 'tar'.
tb	Treebrowser is a useful OPEN LOOK (xview) filesystem browser and manager.
tcl	'Tool Command Language' (tcl) script language.
tcl-devel	'Tool Command Language' (tcl) script language, development part with man-pages.
tclx	Extensions to 'tcl' and 'tk' for POSIX systems.
tclx-devel	Extensions to 'tcl' and 'tk', development part with man-pages.
tcp_wrappers	Security wrapper for tcp daemons - maximum setting.
tcpdump	'tcpdump' allows reading and logging of individual TCP/IP packets.
tcsh	'tcsh', the extended C shell with manual pages.
termcap	Terminal capability collection for GNU libtermcap.
tetex	TeTeX (TeX) typesetting system and MetaFont font formatter.
texinfo	'texinfo' formatter and info reader.
texinfo-info	Text based standalone 'info' reader.
textutils	GNU text utilities like 'cat', 'cksum', 'head', 'join', 'pr', 'sort', 'split' and 'uniq'.
tgif	Object oriented drawing and construction program with special hyperspace mode.
time	GNU time utility, which allows to determine resource usage such as CPU-time and memory of given program executions.

TABLE 14. Software packages on the Caldera OpenLinux Lite CD-ROM

Package	Description
timetool	RedHat graphical time and date setting tool.
tin	'tin', a news reader with NNTP support.
tix	Collection of many metawidgets, such as notepads, for 'tk'.
tix-devel	Metawidgets for tk, development part with man-pages.
tk	'Tk' X interface toolkit for 'Tcl'.
tk-devel	'Tk' toolkit for 'Tcl', development part with man-pages.
tkinfo	Tk/tcl based GNU Info viewer.
tkman	Manual page browser with Tk frontend.
tksysv	X/Tk based System-V 'runlevel' editor.
traceroute	Traces the route that packets take over a TCP/IP network.
tracker	Plays Amiga MOD sound files.
transfig	Converts '.fig' files (such as those from xfig) to other graphic formats.
trn	A threaded news reader with NNTP support.
trojka	A falling blocks game similar to xjewels or tetris for terminals.
tunelp	Configures kernel parallel port driver.
typhoon	Library and utilities for relational databases.
uemacs	MicroEmacs Fullscreen Editor, a small and compact version of Emacs.
umb-scheme	Scheme interpreter from University of Massachusetts at Boston.

TABLE 14. Software packages on the Caldera OpenLinux Lite CD-ROM

Package	Description
umsdos_progs	The programs for the umsdos filesystem, which allows the installation of a Linux system within a DOS partition.
unarj	A decompressor for '.arj' format archives that are widely used under DOS.
units	Units conversion program.
unzip	'unzip' unpacks '.zip' files such as those made by pkzip under DOS.
usercfg	User and group configuration tool.
util-linux	Various Linux utilities, maintained by Rik Faith.
uucp	Unix to Unix Copy (UUCP) for a mail and news via modem connection. Supports HDB as well as Taylor config files. With extensive documentation and 'uupoll' script from Bodo Bauer.
vga_cardgames	Card games 'klondike', 'oh hell', 'solitaire' and 'spider' the Linux text console.
vga_gamespack	'othello', 'minesweeper' and 'connect-4' for the linux text console.
vga_tetris	SVGAlib based tetris games.
vim	'vim' (vi improved), an extended vi editor with support for European characters.
vim-X11	The 'vim' editor (vi improved) with X support.
vixie-cron	The 'cron' daemon allows processes to be started at a predetermined time.
vlock	'vlock' locks one or more virtual consoles.
vslick	Visual Slick Edit demo version from MicroEdge.
wdiff	GNU word difference finder.

TABLE 14. Software packages on the Caldera OpenLinux Lite CD-ROM

Package	Description
which	Determines which executable would be run based on your PATH variable.
words	English dictionary for ispell.
workman	Graphical (OPEN LOOK) tool for playing audio compact discs including a title management for individual CDs.
woven-docs-LST	Woven Goods Documentation - LST
woven-docs-RedHat	Woven Goods Documentation - RedHat
woven-docs-dlhp	Woven Goods Documentation - dlhp
woven-docs-faq	Woven Goods Documentation - FAQ.
woven-docs-fsstnd	Woven Goods Doc - File System Standard
woven-docs-howto	Woven Goods Documentation - HOWTO.
woven-docs-isdn	Woven Goods Documentation - ISDN
woven-docs-ldp	Woven Goods Documentation - LDP.
woven-docs-llhp	Woven Goods Documentation - llhp
woven-docs-main	Woven Goods Documentation - Main.
woven-docs-usenet	Woven Goods Documentation - UseNet.
woven-docs-wwwhelp	Woven Goods Documentation - WWW Help.
wu-ftpd	Washington University FTP daemon.
x3270	X based 3270 emulator; allows a telnet connection to an IBM host within a X window. Special fonts are used.
xanim	'xanim' is an animation viewer for X which supports many graphic formats.
xarchie	X based browser interface to 'archie' for querying the world wide archie database archives.

TABLE 14. Software packages on the Caldera OpenLinux Lite CD-ROM

Package	Description
xbill	Kill the Bill.
xbl	3D Tetris game.
xbmbrowser	Very useful X based browser for bitmaps and pix-maps.
xboing	Breakout style video game.
xcept-demo	A commercial video text-decoder (BTX/Dx-J) for the X (demo version).
xchomp	PacMan like game for X.
xcolorsel	Utility to display or select colors from the RGB database.
xdaliclock	An X based 'dali' clock.
xdemineur	Another minesweeper game.
xearth	The earth globe as background for X root.
xemacs-base	XEmacs base package. XEmacs is a powerful, extendable Editor requiring X-libraries but by now also capable of running on plain terminals.
xemacs-emul	Emulation of other editors (mainly vi) for XEmacs.
xemacs-energize	The 'energize' package for XEmacs.
xemacs-hyperbole	The 'hyperbole' package for XEmacs.
xemacs-lispprog	Lisp programming environment for XEmacs.
xemacs-mailnews	Mail and news readers for XEmacs.
xemacs-modes	Miscellaneous special modes for XEmacs.
xemacs-oo-browse	Object browser for XEmacs.
xemacs-packages	Miscellaneous packages for XEmacs.
xemacs-www	WWW browser and editor for XEmacs.
xevil	A fast action explicitly violent game for X.

TABLE 14. Software packages on the Caldera OpenLinux Lite CD-ROM

Package	Description
xf-control-panel	Icon panel with admin tools.
xf-panel	XForms based icon panel with group hierachy.
xfig	Menu driven graphic application for drawing and manipulating objects. It is capable to save objects in various graphic formats.
xfishtank	Turns X root background into an aquarium.
xfm	A comprehensive file and application manager for X.
xfmail	A spiffy mail reader and editor.
xfractint	Fractal generation program for many different fractal types.
xgalaga	A Galaga clone for X.
xgammon	Backgammon game for one or two players.
xgopher	X based gopher client.
xjewel	A tetris style game for X.
xlander	Moon landing simulation.
xlispstat	Extensible system for statistical computing and dynamic graphics.
xloadimage	X based image viewer supporting many common graphic formats. Images can be displayed or loaded into the background.
xlockmore	X terminal locking program including many screen-savers.
xmailbox	X based mail notification tool.
xmbase-grok	A simple data base with graphical X frontend.
xmgr	Motif based plotting tool.
xmine	Mine sweeper for X.

TABLE 14. Software packages on the Caldera OpenLinux Lite CD-ROM

Package	Description
xmorph	A morphing program with an X interface.
xmplay	An X MPEG video viewer.
xntp	'xntp' allows a precise time synchonisation utilizing a network and/or radio receivers. Requires TCP/IP in the kernel, an initialized loopback device and a correct time zone (see also ktzset from Torsten Duwe).
xosview	An X based utility for viewing the system resources used. For example main memory or cpu load.
xpaint	'xpaint' is a user friendly program for editing and creating pixmaps and bitmaps.
xpat2	X Patience - various solitaire card games.
xpdf	Portable document format (PDF) viewer for X.
xpilot	Arcade style flying game.
xpm	The Xpm libraries for displaying pixmaps.
xpm-devel	Development libraries and header files for handling of pixmaps.
xpostit	Electronic pinboard for daily dates and important ideas.
xpuzzles	Various geometry puzzles including Rubik's Cube.
xrn	X based news reader.
xscreensaver	X screen savers.
xselection	Utility to get or set an X selection or cutbuffer property value.
xsnow	Xsnow, for those who want Christmas 12 months of the year.
xsysinfo	A performance meter for X.
xtar	Motif based 'tar' tool.

TABLE 14. Software packages on the Caldera OpenLinux Lite CD-ROM

Package	Description
xteddy	The cuddly teddy bear for X - a real must for everyone!
xterm-color	ANSI (color) version of the 'xterm' terminal emulator.
xtetris	X version of tetris.
xtoolwait	Delayed X application launcher.
xtrojka	A falling blocks game similar to xjewels or tetris for X.
xv	Great image viewer/browser for most graphic formats (shareware).
xview	XView library and OpenLook interface for X.
xview-devel	Header files and static libraries for XView application development.
xwatch	A watchdog application for log files.
xwpe	Integrated X-Window programming environment.
xwpick	'xwpick' is a screen grabber which saves X windows and backgrounds in various formats.
xxgdb	'xxgdb' is a graphical user interface for the GNU debugger 'gdb'.
ytalk	Uses internet talk protocol to create multiuser chat sessions.
zapem	A space invaders like game.
zgv	Console viewer for many graphics formats.
zip	'zip', a compression program.
zlib	The un-/compression library zlib.
zlib-devel	Static version and header files for zlib.
zoneinfo	Time zone utilities and data.

TABLE 14. Software packages on the Caldera OpenLinux Lite CD-ROM

Package	Description
zsh	zsh shell.
zz_3dlook	3D look for all X applications.

Printing Usage HOWTO

The Linux Printing Usage HOWTO by Mark Komarinski
<markk@auratek.com> v1.2.1, 24 March 1997

1. Introduction

This document describes how to use the line printer spooling system provided with the Linux operating system. This HOWTO is the supplementary document to the Linux Printing Setup HOWTO, which discusses the installation and setup of the Linux printing system. The material presented in this HOWTO should be equally relevent for all flavors of the BSD operating system in addition to the Linux operating system.

1.1. Linux Printing HOWTO History

Note from Mark Komarinski <markk@auratek.com>:

I'd like to thank Matt Foster for doing a lot of work in the re-write of this HOWTO. I'm keeping his style, and adding when necessary to keep everything updated.

Note from Matt Foster <mwf@engr.uark.edu>:

This version of the Linux Printing HOWTO is a complete rewrite of the one originally written by Grant Taylor <grant@god.tufts.edu> and Brian McCauley <B.A.McCauley@bham.ac.uk>. I have tried to keep with the coverage of material presented by Grant and Brian's HOWTO, but I have drastically modified the style of presentation and the depth of material covered. I feel that this makes the HOWTO more complete and easier to read. I can only hope that you agree.

1.2. Version History

*   v1.2.1

    updates, some changes for Dr. Linux publication

*   v1.2

    Windows Printers

    Changing max size of print files

*   v1.11

    new maintainter!

    Added lpc info

    Added some info for troubleshooting

    A start on printing graphics files!

*   v1.1

    revised some of the wording

    developed section on PostScript printing

    attempted to clarify some of the examples 8-)

    fleshed the discussion of the basic Linux printing utilities

*   v1.0

    initial public release of the Printing Usage HOWTO

1.3. Copyrights and Trademarks

Some names mentioned in this HOWTO are claimed as copyrights and/or trademarks of certain persons and/or companies. These names appear in full or initial caps in this HOWTO.

If you have questions, please contact Greg Hankins, the Linux HOWTO coordinator, at <gregh@sunsite.unc.edu>. You may finger this address for phone number and additional contact information.

1.4. Downloading the Linux Printing HOWTOs

I recommend that if you want to print a copy of this HOWTO that you download the PostScript version. It is formatted in a fashion that is aesthetically appealing and easier to read. You can get the PostScript version from one of the many Linux distribution sites (such as SunSITE "").

1.5. Feedback

Questions, comments, or corrections for this HOWTO may be directed to <markk@auratek.com>.

1.6. Acknowledgments

Thanks go out to all of the people who took the time to read the alpha version of this HOWTO and respond with many helpful comments and suggestions---some of you may see your comments reflected in the version.

I'd also like to thank Matt Foster who did the original re-write.

2. Printing Under Linux

This section discusses how to print files, examine the print queue, remove jobs from the print queue, format files before printing them, and configure your printing environment.

2.1. History of Linux Printing

The Linux printing system---the lp system---is a port of the source code written by the Regents of the University of California for the Berkeley Software Distribution version of the UNIX operating system.

2.2. Printing a File Using lpr

By far, the most simplistic way to print in the Linux operating system is to send the file to be printed directly to the printing device. One way to do this is to use the cat command. As the root user, one could do something like

```
# cat thesis.txt > /dev/lp
```

In this case, /dev/lp is a symbolic link to the actual printing device---be it a dot-matrix, laser printer, typesetter, or plotter. (See ln(1) for more information on symbolic links.)

For the purpose of security, only the root user and users in the same group as the print daemon are able to write directly to the printer. This is why commands such as lpr, lprm, and lpq have to be used to access the printer.

Because of this, users have to use lpr to print a file. The lpr command takes care of all the initial work needed to print the file, and then it hands control over to another program, lpd, the line printing daemon. The line printing daemon then tells the printer how to print the file.

When lpr is executed, it first copies the specified file to a certain directory (the spool directory) where the file remains until lpd prints it. Once lpd is told that there is a file to print, it will spawn a copy of itself (what we programmers call forking). This copy will print our file while the original copy waits for more requests. This allows for multiple jobs to be queued at once.

The syntax of lpr(1) is a very familiar one,

```
$ lpr [ options ] [
filename ... ]
```

If filename is not specified, lpr expects input to come from standard input (usually the keyboard, or another program's output). This enables the user to redirect a command's output to the print spooler. As such,

```
$ cat thesis.txt |
lpr
```

or,

```
$ pr -160 the-
sis.txt | lpr
```

The lpr command accepts several command-line arguments that allow a user to control how it works. Some of the most widely used arguments are: -Pprinter specifies the printer to use, -h

suppresses printing of the burst page, -s creates a symbolic link instead of copying the file to the spool directory (useful for large files), and -#num specifies the number of copies to print. An example interaction with lpr might be something like

```
$ lpr -#2 -sP dj
thesis.txt
```

This command will create a symbolic link to the file thesis.txt in the spool directory for the printer named dj, where it would be processed by lpd. It would then print a second copy of thesis.txt.

For a listing of all the options that lpr will recognize, see lpr(1).

2.3. Viewing the Print Queue with lpq

To view the contents of the print queue, use the lpq command. Issued without arguments, it returns the contents of the default printer's queue.

The returned output of lpq can be useful for many purposes.

```
$ lpq lp is ready
and printing Rank
Owner Job Files
Total Size active
mwf 31 thesis.txt
682048 bytes
```

2.4. Canceling a Print Job Using

lprm

Another useful feature of any printing system is the ability to cancel a job that has been previously queued. To do this, use lprm.

```
$ lprm -
```

The above command cancels all of the print jobs that are owned by the user who issued the command. A single print job can be canceled by first getting the job number as reported by lpq and then giving that number to lprm. For example,

```
$ lprm 31
```

would cancel job 31 (thesis.txt) on the default printer.

2.5. Controlling the lpd program with lpc

The lpc(8) program is used to control the printers that lpd serves. you can enable or disable a printer or its queues, rearrange entries within a queue, and get a status report on the printers and their queues. Lpc is mostly used in a setup where there are multiple printers hanging off one machine.

```
$ lpc
```

The above will start the lpc program. By default, this enters you into an interactive mode, and you can begin issuing commands. The other option is to issue an lpc command on the command line.

```
$ lpc status all
```

A list of the available commands are in the lpd man page, but here are a few of the major commands you'll want to know about. Any commands marked with option can either be a printer name (lp, print, etc) or the keyword all, which means all printers.

- disable option - prevents any new printer job from being entered
- down option - disables all printing on the printer
- enable option - allow new jobs to enter the print queue
- quit (or exit) - leave lpc
- restart option - restarts lpd for that printer

- status option - print status of printer
- up option - enable everything and start a new lpd

2.6. The RedHat printtool

Just a quick note here on RedHat's amazing printtool program. It seems to do everything that a magicfilter would do. RedHat already installs many of the programs to do the filtering. Here's how I have my printer set up under RH 4.0 with an HP LJ 4L connected to my parallel port.

1. **Become root and fire up printtool (if you su'ed, you remembered to SETENV DISPLAY :0.0 and xhost +, right?)**

2. **Click "Add", and hit "OK" for a local printer.**

3. **Fill in the printer device (/dev/lp1 for me)**

4. **Fill in the input filter - Select a printer type, resolution, and paper size (ljet4, 300x300, and letter)**

5. **Hit "OK" all the way back, and restart the lpd.**

Just like rolling an /etc/printcap file by hand, you can have multiple printer definitions for each physical printer. One for

different paper sizes, resolutions, etc.

3. Printing files

This section covers printing the kinda of files that you'll run across in a Linux setup.

3.1. Printing graphics files

Printing graphics files through a printer usually depends on the kind of graphics you're converting, and the kind of printer you want to send to. Dot matrix is usually out of the question due to differences in the way dot-matrix handles graphics. Your best bet in this situation is to see if your printer is compatable with an Epson or an IBM ProPrinter, then convert the graphics file to PostScript, then use Ghostscript (see next section) to print the graphics.

If you have a laser printer, things are a bit easier since many are compatable with PCL. This now gives you a few options. Some programs may output directly in PCL. If not, programs like NetPBM can convert into PCL. Last option is to use ghostscript (see next section).

Your absolutely best option is to install packages like NetPBM and Ghostscript then installing a magic filter to process the graphics files automagically.

3.2. Printing PostScript files

Printing PostScript files on a printer that has a PostScript interpreter is simple; just use lpr, and the printer will take care of all of the details for you. For those of us that don't have printers with PostScript capabilities, we have to resort to other means. Luckily, there are programs available that can make sense of PostScript, and translate it into a language that most printers will understand. Probably the most well known of these programs is Ghostscript.

Ghostscript's responsibility is to convert all of the descriptions in a PostScript file to commands that the printer will understand. To print a PostScript file using Ghostscript, you might do something like

```
$ gs -dSAFER -dNOPAUSE -sDEVICE=deskjet -sOutput-
File=\|lpr thesis.ps
```

Notice in the above example that we are actually piping the output of Ghostscript to the lpr command by using the -sOutputFile option.

Ghostview is an interface to Ghostscript for the X Window System. It allows you to preview a PostScript file before you print it. Ghostview and Ghostscript can both be swiped from "".

3.3. Printing PDF files

Adobe has released an Acrobat reader for Linux, and it's available on the Adobe home page "". Its predecessor, xpdf, is also available. Both should print to a postscript device.

3.4. Printing TeX files

One of the easiest ways to print TeX files is to convert them to PostScript and then print them using Ghostscript. To do this, you first need to convert them from TeX to a format known as DVI (which stands for device-independent). You can do this with the tex(1) command. Then you need to convert the DVI file to a Post-Script file using dvips. All of this would look like the following when typed in.

```
$ tex thesis.tex $
dvips thesis.dvi
```

Now you are ready to print the resulting PostScript file as described above.

3.5. Printing troff formatted files

```
$ groff -Tascii
thesis.tr | lpr
```

or, if you prefer,

```
$ groff thesis.tr
> thesis.ps
```

and then print the PostScript file as described above.

3.6. Printing man pages

```
$ man man | col -b |
lpr
```

The man pages contain pre-formatted troff data, so we have to strip out any highlighting, underlines, etc. The 'col' program does this just nicely, and since we're piping data, the man program won't use more.

4. Miscellaneous Items

4.1. Formatting Before Printing

Since most ASCII files are not formatted for printing, it is useful to format them in some way before they are actually printed. This may include putting a title and page number on each page, setting the margins, double spacing, indenting, or printing a file in multiple columns. A common way to do this is to use a print preprocessor such as pr.

```
$ pr +4 -d -h"Ph.D.
Thesis, 2nd Draft"
-l60 thesis.txt |
lpr
```

In the above example, pr would take the file thesis.txt and skip the first three pages (+4), set the page length to sixty lines (-l60), double space the output (-d), and add the phrase "Ph.D. Thesis, 2nd Draft" to the top of each page (-h). Lpr would then queue pr's output. See its on-line manual page for more information on using pr.

4.2. The PRINTER Environment Variables

All of the commands in the Linux printing system accept the -P option. This option allows the user to specify which printer to use for output. If a user doesn't specify which printer to use, then the default printer will be assumed as the output device.

Instead of having to specify a printer to use every time that you print, you can set the PRINTER environment variable to the name of the printer that you want to use. This is accomplished in different ways for each shell. For bash you can do this with

```
$ PRINTER="printer_name"; export PRINTER
```

and csh, you can do it with

```
% setenv PRINTER "printer_name"
```

These commands can be placed in your login scripts (.profile for bash, or .cshrc for csh), or issued on the command-line. (See bash(1) and csh(1) for more information on environment variables.)

5. Answers to Frequently Asked Questions

Q1. How do I prevent the staircase effect?

A1. The staircase effect is caused by the way some printers expect lines to be terminated. Some printers want lines that end with a carriage-return/line-feed sequence (DOS-style) instead of the line-feed sequence used for UNIX-type systems. The easiest way to fix this is to see if your printer can switch between the two styles somehow---either by flipping a DIP switch, or by sending an escape sequence at the start of each print job. To do the latter, you need to create a filter (see Q2).

A quick fix is to use a filter on the command-line. An example of this might be

```
$ cat thesis.txt | todos | lpr
```

Q2. *What is a filter?*

A2. A filter is a program that reads from standard input (stdin), performs some action on this input, and writes to standard output (stdout). Filters are used for a lot of things, including text processing.

Q3. *What is a magic filter?*

A3. A magic filter is a filter that performs an action based on a file's type. For example, if the file is a plain, text file, it would simply print the file using the normal methods. If the file is a PostScript file, or any other format, it would print it using another method (ghostscript). Two examples of this is magicfilter and APSfilter. One caveat of these filters is that the appropriate programs have to be installed before you install the filter.

The reason for this is that when the magicfilter gets installed, it queries your system for specific programs (such as ghostscript - if it finds it, then it knows it can handle PostScript data), then builds itself based on what it finds. To handle all the printer files, you should probably have at least the following installed:

- GhostScript
- TeX
- NetPBM
- jpeg utilities
- gzip

Q4. *What about the Windows Printing System? Will Linux work with that?*

A4. Maybe. Printers that accept only the WPS commands will not work with Linux. Printers that accept WPS and other commands (such as the Canon BJC 610) will work, as long as they're set to something other than WPS format. Other printers, such as some HP DeskJet 820Cxi/Cse, will *not* work with Linux. That being said, Linux can act as a print server (See Samba) for Win95 machines, since Win95 has drivers for those printers.

Q5. *What kinda cheey system is this? I can't print more than 6 pages or else I get a "file too large" error.*

A5. One of the options in the /etc/printcap file relates to the maximum size of a print file. The default is 1000 disk blocks (about 500k?). For PostScript files and the like, this will give you maybe 6-8 pages with graphics and all. Be sure to add the following line in the printer definition:

```
mx=0
```

The primary reason for this is to keep the spool partition from get ting filled. There is another way to do it, by making lpr create a soft link from the spool directory to your print file. But you have to remember to add the -s option to lpr every time.

6. Troubleshooting

This section covers some common things that can go wrong with your printing system.

If your printer doesn't work:

- Do other print jobs work? (application problem?)
- Is lpd running? (check it using lpc) (print controller?)
- Can root send something directly to the printer? (print services?)
- Can you print from DOS? (cable/printer problem?)

Answering these questions can help find a solution.

Send other suggestions for this section to <markk@auratek.com>.

7. References

This is a section of references on the Linux printing system. I have tried to keep the references section of this HOWTO as focused as possible. If you feel that I have forgotten a significant reference work, please do not hesitate to contact me.

Before you post your question to a USENET group, consider the following:

- Is the printer accepting jobs? (Use lpc(8) to verify.)
- Is the answer to your question covered in this HOWTO or Grant Taylor's Printing HOWTO?

If any of the above are true, you may want to think twice before you post your question. And, when you do finally post to a newsgroup, try to include pertinent information. Try not to just say something like, "I'm having trouble with lpr, please help." These types of posts will most definitely be ignored by many. Also try to include the kernel version that you're running, how the error occured, and, if any, the specific error message that the system returned. On-Line Manual Pages

- cat(1) concatenate and print files
- dvips(1) convert a TeX DVI file to PostScript

- ghostview(1) view PostScript documents using Ghostscript
- groff(1) front-end for the groff document formatting system
- gs(1) Ghostscript interpreter/ viewer
- lpc(8) line printer control program
- lpd(8) line printer spooler daemon
- lpq(1) spool queue examination program
- lpr(1) off-line printer
- lprm(1) remove jobs from the line printer spooling queue
- pr(1) convert text files for printing
- tex(1) text formatting and typesetting
- USENET newsgroups
- comp.os.linux.* a plethora of information on Linux
- comp.unix.* discussions relating to the UNIX operating system

License Statements

This Appendix contains licensing information for the components of your OpenLinux™ Lite CD-ROM.

Many of the software packages included on the Caldera OpenLinux™ Lite CD-ROM are distributed under the Gnu General Public License (Gnu GPL), which is reprinted below, or other licenses that allow code to be distributed. Consult the appropriate license statement in this Appendix, or in the source code or documentation for additional details regarding any component that you would like to re-distribute.

Some other components have been licensed by Caldera from commercial software development companies. These components constitute Caldera's value-add to the Linux operating system. They are *not* distributed under the Gnu GPL, and *may not be re-distributed*. These components, which are marked by an asterisk (*) in the table of software packages that begins on page 190, are distributed under the Caldera End-User license agreement in this Appendix.

If you are aware of other license statements that should be included here, but have been overlooked, we would appreciate your contacting us.

Caldera End-User License Agreement

BY OPENING THE CD-ROM PACKAGE, YOU ARE CONSENTING TO BE BOUND BY AND ARE BECOMING A PARTY TO THIS AGREEMENT. IF YOU DO NOT AGREE TO ALL OF THE TERMS OF THIS AGREEMENT, RETURN THE COMPLETE PACKAGE UNOPENED TO THE PLACE OF PURCHASE FOR A FULL REFUND.

CALDERA OPENLINUX LITE END-USER LICENSE AGREEMENT

GRANT. Caldera, Inc. ("Caldera") hereby grants you a non-exclusive license to use its accompanying software product ("Software") and accompanying documentation ("Documentation") on the following terms:

You may:

- use the Software on any single computer;
- use the Software on a second computer so long as the first and second computers are not used simultaneously; or
- copy the Software for archival purposes, provided any copy must contain all of the original Software's proprietary notices.

You may not:

- permit other individuals to use the Software except under the terms listed above;
- modify, translate, reverse engineer, decompile, disassemble (except to the extent applicable laws specifically prohibit such restriction), or create derivative works based on the Software;
- copy the Software (except for back-up purposes);
- rent, lease, transfer or otherwise transfer rights to the Software; or
- remove any proprietary notices or labels on the Software.

SOFTWARE. If you receive your first copy of the Software electronically, and a second copy on media, the second copy may be used for archival purposes only. This license does not grant you any right to any enhancement or update.

TITLE. Title, ownership rights, and intellectual property rights in and to the Software covered by this agreement shall remain in Caldera and/or its suppliers. The Software is protected by the copyright laws of the United States and international copyright treaties. Title, ownership rights, and intellectual property rights in and to the content accessed through the Software is the property of the applicable content owner and may be protected by applicable copyright or other law. This License gives you no rights to such content.

LIMITED WARRANTY. Caldera warrants that for a period of ninety (90) days from the date of acquisition, the Software, if operated as directed, will substantially achieve the functionality described in the Documentation. Caldera does not warrant, however, that your use of the Software will be uninterrupted or that the operation of the Software will be error-free or secure and hereby disclaims any and all liability on account thereof. In addition, the security mechanisms implemented by the Software have inherent limitations, and you must determine that the Software sufficiently meets your requirements. Caldera also warrants that the media containing the Software, if provided by Caldera, is free from defects in material and workmanship and will so remain for ninety (90) days from the date you acquired the Software. Caldera's sole liability for any breach of this warranty shall be, in Caldera's sole discretion: (i) to replace your defective media; or (ii) to advise you how to achieve substantially the same functionality with the Software as described in the Documentation through a procedure different from that set forth in the Documentation; or (iii) if the above remedies are impracticable, to refund the license fee you paid for the Software. Repaired, corrected, or replaced Software and Documentation shall be covered by this limited warranty for the period remaining under the warranty that covered the original Software, or if longer, for thirty (30) days after the date (a) of shipment to you of the repaired or replaced Software, or (b) Caldera advised you how to operate the Software so as to achieve the functionality described in the Documentation. Only if you inform Caldera of your problem with the Software during the applicable warranty period and provide evidence of the date you acquired the Software will Caldera be obligated to honor this warranty. Caldera will use reasonable commercial efforts to repair, replace, advise, or refund pursuant to the foregoing warranty within 30 days of being so notified.

THIS IS A LIMITED WARRANTY AND IT IS THE ONLY WARRANTY MADE BY CALDERA. CALDERA MAKES NO OTHER EXPRESS WARRANTY AND NO WARRANTY OR CONDITION OF NONINFRINGEMENT OF THIRD PARTIES' RIGHTS. THE DURATION OF IMPLIED WARRANTIES, INCLUDING WITHOUT L'MITATION, WARRANTIES OF MERCHANTABILITY AND OF FITNESS FOR A PARTICULAR PURPOSE, IS LIMITED TO THE ABOVE LIMITED WARRANTY PERIOD; SOME STATES DO NOT ALLOW LIMITATIONS ON HOW LONG AN IMPLIED WARRANTY LASTS, SO THESE LIMITATIONS MAY NOT APPLY TO YOU. NO CALDERA DEALER, AGENT, OR EMPLOYEE IS AUTHORIZED TO MAKE ANY MODIFICATIONS, EXTENSIONS, OR ADDITIONS TO THIS WARRANTY. If any modifications are made to the Software by you during the warranty period; if the media is subjected to accident, abuse, or improper use; or if you violate the terms of this Agreement, then this warranty shall immediately be terminated. This warranty shall not apply if the Software is used on or in conjunction with hardware or Software other than the unmodified version of hardware and Software with which the Software was designed to be used as described in the Documentation.

THIS WARRANTY GIVES YOU SPECIFIC LEGAL RIGHTS, AND YOU MAY HAVE OTHER LEGAL RIGHTS THAT VARY FROM STATE TO STATE OR BY JURISDICTION.

LIMITATION OF LIABILITY. UNDER NO CIRCUMSTANCES AND UNDER NO LEGAL THEORY, TORT, CONTRACT, OR OTHERWISE, SHALL CALDERA OR ITS SUPPLIERS OR RESELLERS BE LIABLE TO YOU OR ANY OTHER PERSON FOR

ANY INDIRECT, SPECIAL, INCIDENTAL, OR CONSEQUENTIAL DAMAGES OF ANY CHARACTER INCLUDING, WITHOUT LIMITATION, DAMAGES FOR LOSS OF GOODWILL, WORK STOPPAGE, COMPUTER FAILURE OR MALFUNCTION, OR ANY AND ALL OTHER COMMERCIAL DAMAGES OR LOSSES, OR FOR ANY DAMAGES IN EXCESS OF CALDERA'S LIST PRICE FOR A LICENSE TO THE SOFTWARE AND DOCUMENTATION, EVEN IF CALDERA SHALL HAVE BEEN INFORMED OF THE POSSIBILITY OF SUCH DAMAGES, OR FOR ANY CLAIM BY ANY OTHER PARTY. THIS LIMITATION OF LIABILITY SHALL NOT APPLY TO LIABILITY FOR DEATH OR PERSONAL INJURY TO THE EXTENT APPLICABLE LAW PROHIBITS SUCH LIMITATION. FURTHERMORE, SOME STATES DO NOT ALLOW THE EXCLUSION OR LIMITATION OF INCIDENTAL OR CONSEQUENTIAL DAMAGES, SO THIS LIMITATION AND EXCLUSION MAY NOT APPLY TO YOU.

TERMINATION. This license will terminate automatically if you fail to comply with the limitations described above. On termination, you must destroy all copies of the Software and Documentation.

EXPORT CONTROLS. None of the Software or underlying information or technology may be downloaded or otherwise exported or reexported (i) into (or to a national or resident of) Cuba, Iraq, Libya, Yugoslavia, North Korea, Iran, Syria or any other country to which the U.S. has embargoed goods; or (ii) to anyone on the U.S. Treasury Department's list of Specially Designated Nationals or the U.S. Commerce Department's Table of Deny Orders. By using the Software, you are agreeing to the foregoing and you are representing and warranting that you are not located in, under the control of, or a national or resident of any such country or on any such list.

In addition, if the licensed Software is identified as a not-for-export product (for example, on the box, media, or in the installation process), then the following applies: EXCEPT FOR EXPORT TO CANADA FOR USE IN CANADA BY CANADIAN CITIZENS, THE

SOFTWARE AND ANY UNDERLYING TECHNOLOGY MAY NOT BE EXPORTED OUTSIDE THE UNITED STATES OR TO ANY FOREIGN ENTITY OR "FOREIGN PERSON" AS DEFINED BY U.S. GOVERNMENT REGULATIONS, INCLUDING WITHOUT LIMITATION, ANYONE WHO IS NOT A CITIZEN, NATIONAL, OR LAWFUL PERMANENT RESIDENT OF THE UNITED STATES. BY USING THE SOFTWARE, YOU ARE AGREEING TO THE FOREGOING AND YOU ARE WARRANTING THAT YOU ARE NOT A "FOREIGN PERSON" OR UNDER THE CONTROL OF A FOREIGN PERSON.

MISCELLANEOUS. This Agreement represents the complete agreement concerning this license between the parties and supersedes all prior agreements and representations between them. It may be amended only by a writing executed by both parties. If any provision of this Agreement is held to be unenforceable for any reason, such provision shall be reformed only to the extent necessary to make it enforceable. This Agreement shall be governed by and construed under Utah law as such law applies to agreements between Utah residents entered into and to be performed within Utah, except as governed by Federal law. The application of the United Nations Convention of Contracts for the International Sale of Goods is expressly excluded.

U.S. Government Restricted Rights. Use, duplication or disclosure by the Government is subject to restrictions set forth in subparagraphs (a) through (d) of the Commercial Computer-Restricted Rights clause at FAR 52.227-19 when applicable, or in subparagraph (c)(1)(ii) of the Rights in Technical Data and Computer Software clause at DFARS 252.227-7013, and in similar clauses in the NASA FAR Supplement. Contractor/manufacturer is Caldera, Inc. 931 West Center Street, Orem, Utah, 84057.

GNU General Public License

Version 2, June 1991

Copyright © 1989, 1991 Free Software Foundation, Inc. 675 Mass Ave, Cambridge, MA 02139, USA

Everyone is permitted to copy and distribute verbatim copies of this license document, but changing it is not allowed.

Preamble

The licenses for most software are designed to take away your freedom to share and change it. By contrast, the GNU General Public License is intended to guarantee your freedom to share and change free software-- to make sure the software is free for all its users. This General Public License applies to most of the Free Software Foundation's software and to any other program whose authors commit to using it. (Some other Free Software Foundation software is covered by the GNU Library General Public License instead.) You can apply it to your programs, too.

When we speak of free software, we are referring to freedom, not price. Our General Public Licenses are designed to make sure that you have the freedom to distribute copies of free software (and charge for this service if you wish), that you receive source code or can get it if you want it, that you can change the software or use pieces of it in new free programs; and that you know you can do these things.

To protect your rights, we need to make restrictions that forbid anyone to deny you these rights or to ask you to surrender the rights. These restrictions translate to certain responsibilities for you if you distribute copies of the software, or if you modify it.

For example, if you distribute copies of such a program, whether gratis or for a fee, you must give the recipients all the rights that you have. You must make sure that they, too, receive or can get the source code. And you must show them these terms so they know their rights.

We protect your rights with two steps: (1) copyright the software, and (2) offer you this license which gives you legal permission to copy, distribute and/or modify the software.

Also, for each author's protection and ours, we want to make certain that everyone understands that there is no warranty for this free software. If the software is modified by someone else and passed on, we want its recipients to know that what they have is not the original, so that any problems introduced by others will not reflect on the original authors' reputations.

Finally, any free program is threatened constantly by software patents. We wish to avoid the danger that redistributors of a free program will individually obtain patent licenses, in effect making the program proprietary. To prevent this, we have made it clear that any patent must be licensed for everyone's free use or not licensed at all.

The precise terms and conditions for copying, distribution and modification follow.

GNU GENERAL PUBLIC LICENSE

TERMS AND CONDITIONS FOR COPYING, DISTRIBUTION AND MODIFICATION

0.   This License applies to any program or other work which contains a notice placed by the copyright holder saying it may be distributed under the terms of this General Public License. The "Program", below, refers to any such program or work, and a "work based on the Program" means either the Program or any derivative work under copyright law: that is to say, a work containing the Program or a portion of it, either verbatim or with modifications and/or translated into another language. (Hereinafter, translation is included without limitation in the term "modification".) Each licensee is addressed as "you".

Activities other than copying, distribution and modification are not covered by this License; they are outside its scope. The act of running the Program is not restricted, and the output from the Program is covered only if its contents constitute a work based on the Program (independent of having been made by running the Program). Whether that is true depends on what the Program does.

1. You may copy and distribute verbatim copies of the Program's source code as you receive it, in any medium, provided that you conspicuously and appropriately publish on each copy an appropriate copyright notice and disclaimer of warranty; keep intact all the notices that refer to this License and to the absence of any warranty; and give any other recipients of the Program a copy of this License along with the Program.

   You may charge a fee for the physical act of transferring a copy, and you may at your option offer warranty protection in exchange for a fee.

2. You may modify your copy or copies of the Program or any portion of it, thus forming a work based on the Program, and copy and distribute such modifications or work under the terms of Section 1 above, provided that you also meet all of these conditions:

   a. You must cause the modified files to carry prominent notices stating that you changed the files and the date of any change.

   b. You must cause any work that you distribute or publish, that in whole or in part contains or is derived from the Program or any part thereof, to be licensed as a whole at no charge to all third parties under the terms of this License.

   c. If the modified program normally reads commands interactively when run, you must cause it, when started running for such interactive use in the most ordinary way, to print or display an announcement including an appropriate copyright notice and a notice that there is no warranty (or else, saying that you provide a warranty) and that users may redistribute the program under these conditions, and telling the user how to view a copy of this License. (Exception: if the Program itself is interactive but does not normally print such an announcement, your work based on the Program is not required to print an announcement.)

These requirements apply to the modified work as a whole. If identifiable sections of that work are not derived from the Program, and can be reasonably considered independent and separate works in themselves, then this License, and its terms, do not apply to those sections when you distribute them as separate works. But when you distribute the same sections as part of a whole which is a work based on the Program, the distribution of the whole must be on the terms of this License, whose permissions for other licensees extend to the entire whole, and thus to each and every part regardless of who wrote it.

Thus, it is not the intent of this section to claim rights or contest your rights to work written entirely by you; rather, the intent is to exercise the right to control the distribution of derivative or collective works based on the Program.

In addition, mere aggregation of another work not based on the Program with the Program (or with a work based on the Program) on a volume of a storage or distribution medium does not bring the other work under the scope of this License.

3.   You may copy and distribute the Program (or a work based on it, under Section 2) in object code or executable form under the terms of Sections 1 and 2 above provided that you also do one of the following:

a.   Accompany it with the complete corresponding machine-readable source code, which must be distributed under the terms of Sections 1 and 2 above on a medium customarily used for software interchange; or,

b.   Accompany it with a written offer, valid for at least three years, to give any third party, for a charge no more than your cost of physically performing source distribution, a complete machine-readable copy of the corresponding source code, to be distributed under the terms of Sections 1 and 2 above on a medium customarily used for software interchange; or,

c.   Accompany it with the information you received as to the offer to distribute corresponding source code. (This alternative is allowed only for noncommercial distribution and only if you received the program in object code or executable form with such an offer, in accord with Subsection b above.)

The source code for a work means the preferred form of the work for making modifications to it. For an executable work, complete source code means all the source code for all modules it contains, plus any associated interface definition files, plus the scripts used to control compilation and installation of the executable. However, as a special exception, the source code distributed need not include anything that is normally distributed (in either source or binary form) with the major components (compiler, kernel, and so on) of the operating system on which the executable runs, unless that component itself accompanies the executable.

If distribution of executable or object code is made by offering access to copy from a designated place, then offering equivalent access to copy the source code from the same place counts as distribution of the source code, even though third parties are not compelled to copy the source along with the object code.

4. You may not copy, modify, sublicense, or distribute the Program except as expressly provided under this License. Any attempt otherwise to copy, modify, sublicense or distribute the Program is void, and will automatically terminate your rights under this License.

   However, parties who have received copies, or rights, from you under this License will not have their licenses terminated so long as such parties remain in full compliance.

5. You are not required to accept this License, since you have not signed it. However, nothing else grants you permission to modify or distribute the Program or its derivative works. These actions are prohibited by law if you do not accept this License. Therefore, by modifying or distributing the Program (or any work based on the Program), you indicate your acceptance of this License to do so, and all its terms and conditions for copying, distributing or modifying the Program or works based on it.

6. Each time you redistribute the Program (or any work based on the Program), the recipient automatically receives a license from the original licensor to copy, distribute or modify the Program subject to these terms and conditions. You may not impose any further restrictions on the recipients' exercise of the rights granted herein. You are not responsible for enforcing compliance by third parties to this License.

7. If, as a consequence of a court judgment or allegation of patent infringement or for any other reason (not limited to patent issues), conditions are imposed on you (whether by court order, agreement or

otherwise) that contradict the conditions of this License, they do not excuse you from the conditions of this License. If you cannot distribute so as to satisfy simultaneously your obligations under this License and any other pertinent obligations, then as a consequence you may not distribute the Program at all. For example, if a patent license would not permit royalty-free redistribution of the Program by all those who receive copies directly or indirectly through you, then the only way you could satisfy both it and this License would be to refrain entirely from distribution of the Program.

If any portion of this section is held invalid or unenforceable under any particular circumstance, the balance of the section is intended to apply and the section as a whole is intended to apply in other circumstances.

It is not the purpose of this section to induce you to infringe any patents or other property right claims or to contest validity of any such claims; this section has the sole purpose of protecting the integrity of the free software distribution system, which is implemented by public license practices. Many people have made generous contributions to the wide range of software distributed through that system in reliance on consistent application of that system; it is up to the author/donor to decide if he or she is willing to distribute software through any other system and a licensee cannot impose that choice.

This section is intended to make thoroughly clear what is believed to be a consequence of the rest of this License.

8. If the distribution and/or use of the Program is restricted in certain countries either by patents or by copyrighted interfaces, the original copyright holder who places the Program under this License may add an explicit geographical distribution limitation excluding those countries, so that distribution is permitted only in or among countries not thus excluded. In such case, this License incorporates the limitation as if written in the body of this License.

9. The Free Software Foundation may publish revised and/or new versions of the General Public License from time to time. Such new versions will be similar in spirit to the present version, but may differ in detail to address new problems or concerns.

Each version is given a distinguishing version number. If the Program specifies a version number of this License which applies to it and "any later version", you have the option of following the terms and conditions either of that version or of any later version published by the Free Software Foundation. If the Program does not specify a version number of this License, you may choose any version ever published by the Free Software Foundation.

10. If you wish to incorporate parts of the Program into other free programs whose distribution conditions are different, write to the author to ask for permission. For software which is copyrighted by the Free Software Foundation, write to the Free Software Foundation; we sometimes make exceptions for this. Our decision will be guided by the two goals of preserving the free status of all derivatives of our free software and of promoting the sharing and reuse of software generally.

NO WARRANTY

11. BECAUSE THE PROGRAM IS LICENSED FREE OF CHARGE, THERE IS NO WARRANTY FOR THE PROGRAM, TO THE EXTENT PERMITTED BY APPLICABLE LAW. EXCEPT WHEN OTHERWISE STATED IN WRITING THE COPYRIGHT HOLDERS AND/OR OTHER PARTIES PROVIDE THE PROGRAM "AS IS" WITHOUT WARRANTY OF ANY KIND, EITHER EXPRESSED OR IMPLIED, INCLUDING, BUT NOT LIMITED TO, THE IMPLIED WARRANTIES OF MERCHANTABILITY AND FITNESS FOR A PARTICULAR PURPOSE. THE ENTIRE RISK AS TO THE QUALITY AND PERFORMANCE OF THE PROGRAM IS WITH YOU. SHOULD THE PROGRAM PROVE DEFECTIVE, YOU ASSUME THE COST OF ALL NECESSARY SERVICING,

REPAIR OR CORRECTION.

12. IN NO EVENT UNLESS REQUIRED BY APPLICABLE LAW OR AGREED TO IN WRITING WILL ANY COPYRIGHT HOLDER, OR ANY OTHER PARTY WHO MAY MODIFY AND/OR REDISTRIBUTE THE PROGRAM AS PERMITTED ABOVE, BE LIABLE TO YOU FOR DAMAGES, INCLUDING ANY GENERAL, SPECIAL, INCIDENTAL OR CONSEQUENTIAL DAMAGES ARISING OUT OF THE USE OR INABILITY TO USE THE PROGRAM (INCLUDING BUT NOT LIMITED TO LOSS OF DATA OR DATA BEING RENDERED INACCURATE OR LOSSES SUSTAINED BY YOU OR THIRD PARTIES OR A FAILURE OF THE PROGRAM TO OPERATE WITH ANY OTHER PROGRAMS), EVEN IF SUCH HOLDER OR OTHER PARTY HAS BEEN ADVISED OF THE POSSIBILITY OF SUCH DAMAGES.

END OF TERMS AND CONDITIONS

University of California Copyright (Berkeley)

Some components of OpenLinux are covered by the following copyright notice:

Copyright © 1989 Regents of the University of California. All rights reserved. Redistribution and use in source and binary forms are permitted provided that the above copyright notice and this paragraph are duplicated in all such forms and that any documentation, advertising materials, and other materials related to such distribution and use acknowledge that the software was developed by the University of California, Berkeley. The name of the University may not be used to endorse or promote products derived from this software without specific prior written permission. THIS SOFTWARE IS PROVIDED "AS IS" AND WITHOUT ANY EXPRESS OR IMPLIED WARRANTIES, INCLUDING, WITHOUT LIMITATION, THE IMPLIED WARRANTIES OF MERCHANTIBILITY AND FITNESS FOR A PARTICULAR PURPOSE.

Index

Introduction to OpenLinux

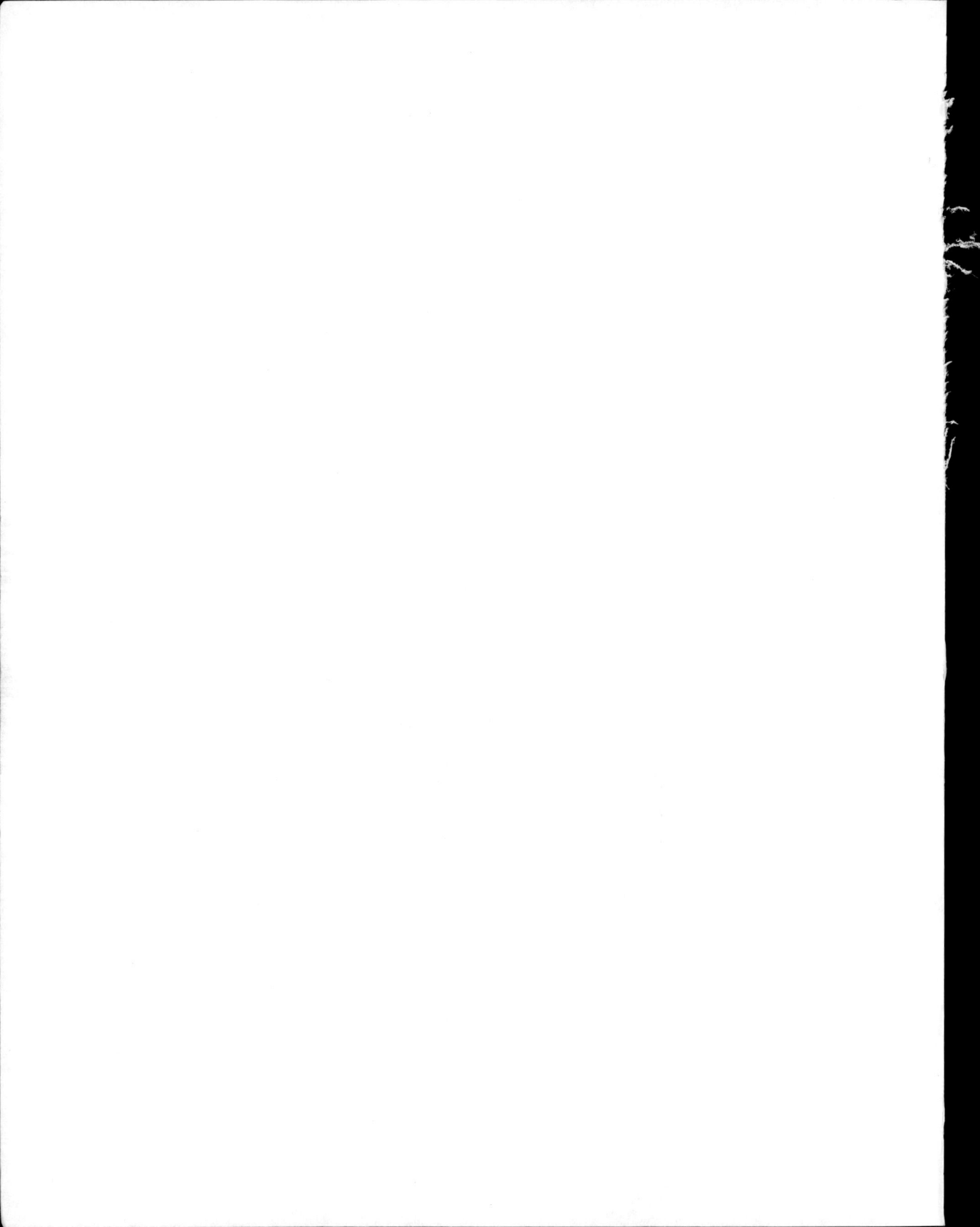